PLANTIFUL

PLANTIFUL

start small,
grow big with 150
plants that spread,
self-sow, and
overwinter

kristin green

timber press
portland • london

CONTENTS

PREFACE

"It is the spectrum, not the color, that makes color worth having, and it is the cycle, not the instant, that makes the day worth living."
—*Henry Mitchell*

For whatever reason any of us are compelled to start growing a garden—and the reasons are at least as varied as our dirt-encrusted fingerprints—eventually or instantly, plants win us over. Captivated by the infinite variety in the shades of green, shapes, textures, and personalities, and spurred by the thrill of any plant's survival under our care, we inevitably develop a craving for more. In part, this book is about building a collection to satisfy that hunger.

It's also about gardening with plants. Some say it takes at least twelve years to create a garden, time for shrubs and trees to mature and for the garden to come into its own. While I understand that every gardener participates in nature's processes in varying degrees

Dark-leaved *Dahlia* 'Moonfire' planted among airy puffs of self-sowing foxtail barley (*Hordeum jubatum*) and feathertop grass (*Pennisetum villosum*) create a richly textured autumn spectacle.

and with different expectations, I don't want to wait that long. I expect my garden to grow.

Six years ago, when I first set foot in my yard, I was so impatient to see a garden grow there that my friends gave me as many extra annual seedlings, perennial divisions, tender-perennial cuttings, and dahlia tubers as I could stuff in hastily made beds. Those starts filled in around the few precious specimen trees, shrubs, and perennials I scrimped for, and loaded my garden's first and subsequent seasons with color, and bird and insect activity. To me, it is established already, and it's a work in progress that gets better all the time. I have been chasing my dream garden long enough to know that it's the chase that keeps me gardening. After all, no garden is ever done.

I know that's true because I make my living tending a mature one. The family that purchased seventy acres on the Narragansett Bay shore in 1895 began planting gardens there immediately and never stopped fine-tuning their dream. Some of the trees at Blithewold Mansion, Gardens & Arboretum, now

a thirty-three-acre nonprofit public garden, are over one hundred years old, others over one hundred feet tall, but the gardens change all the time as gardens do. Plants grow from seed and out from the roots every day of the week. Stems lengthen, leaves unfurl, flowers open, bees visit, hummingbirds bicker, seedheads form, leaves fall, plants die, and the garden staff and volunteers take advantage of every opportunity to help effect transformation.

The stumbling block for a lot of gardeners, me included, is that time keeps changing along with the garden. We have so much to do inside that some of us are spending less time outside. The days feel shorter than ever and 99 percent of us feel pinched financially too. So we all look for shortcuts along the garden's path to maturity. My shortcut, described in this book, involves dirty knees, compost heaps, and propagation. I take the route paved with old-fashioned resourcefulness and engagement with plants that grow, some of them by leaps and bounds, and a hands-on approach to garden design.

Aside from some full days in spring preparing for the season, I spend only as much time as I have—stolen minutes to a couple of hours on Saturday—transforming my own garden because the plants do a lot of the work for me. It might be the momentum of obsession that propels me to wander through it when I do, snips and trowel in hand, determined to make the adjustments that could turn dream into reality, ephemeral as it may be, but it's also how I mark the passage of time, decompress after long work days, and reconnect with my very own patch of the planet. The more time I spend in it, the more time I want to, and days lengthen like magic.

IN THIS BOOK you'll learn how to use, edit, propagate, and choose fifty self-sowers that emerge year after

year in new and surprising combinations. Let self-sowers, also known as volunteers, work for you as ephemeral screens and formal focal points. Allow them to weave through borders and drift into crevices, and press some into service as early-summer groundcovers and weed barriers.

You'll discover fifty spreaders that make it possible to grow more garden than you ever thought your schedule or budget would allow. Plants that spread from their roots and shoots will function as placeholders and fillers that outcompete weeds and give heft to skimpy borders. They can be used to establish a rhythm and to knit one-of-thises-and-thats together. Save for a rainy day by borrowing extra suckers and runners from shrubs and perennials to use as cheap thrillers, spillers, and fillers in containers.

And you'll find out why plants that can't survive our winters don't have to be thrown on the compost at the end of the season. If you have the space—on windowsills, in an enclosed porch, under the cover of a cold frame, or in your cellar—why shouldn't the garden, or at least part of it, follow you in from the cold every year? Treat yourself to richly ornamental bee magnets and hummingbird feeders that are worth the investment because they *can* survive the winter with some protection, indoors or out. The fifty season-extending frost-tender plants profiled in this book are sure to keep your garden active right up until a killing frost, you engaged through the winter, and your wallet stowed the following spring.

GARDENERS ARE USUALLY described as generous but I think evangelistic hits closer to the mark. Most of us cheerleaders would give everything we have and know to anyone who so much as glances in our garden's direction, wanting nothing more in return than to see another dream garden started and the love of the chase passed on to someone else in turn. I would share every plant in my garden with you if I could. Instead, I wrote this. Pass it on.

Mountain mint (*Pycnanthemum muticum*) spreads to help fill an extravagantly planted mixed border.

GARDENING WITH A GENEROUS NATURE

SOME GROUND RULES

A front yard garden tapestry full of self-sowers, spreaders, and keepers. PREVIOUS PAGE Weeds don't stand a chance in these ample late-summer borders generously planted with anise hyssop, dahlias, and tall verbena.

Whoever said that money doesn't grow on trees must not have been a gardener, or didn't yet comprehend just how much nature gives away for free. Gardeners save big when plants grow, especially if they grow quickly, and spread vigorously. I know what you're thinking! But our thrifty great-grandparents could have taught us the value of those plants far too beautiful, useful, and benign to be dismissed as "weeds." Nowadays too, it's the old-school plants, propagation methods, and strategies for extending the season that make the garden wildly interesting and different every year, while still keeping it inexpensive, easy, and more gratifying to perfect. You'll find that it is possible to grow a garden that looks expensive and like too much work, without spending the earth or giving up your day job, when you rise to the challenge of growing nature's worthiest opportunists.

It's easy: simply drop the weight of anxiety and reach for adventurous optimism. Become more interested and invested as your garden grows. As long as you are paying even minimal attention to your garden and the passage of the seasons, plants that self-sow and spread from the roots won't be able to take over, and those that would die without refuge from winter's worst can be kept alive for years instead. Take advantage of these plants' survival mechanisms and use them to hone your garden's design as well as your skills, by shifting plants in, out, and around by the day or season, whenever inspiration strikes. Such creativity is psychologically so much easier—and more rewarding—when there's nothing to lose and everything to gain.

To start cashing in on nature's generosity, cultivate a true, mad love for plants and develop an opportunistic streak yourself. The more intrigued you become, and the more thrill you seek in growing, the more you'll grow. And the more you grow—both in your garden and as a gardener—the more rewarding your garden will be. Arm yourself with a basic understanding of plant's life cycles, reproductive mechanisms, and their potential liabilities. Then discover the joy in serendipitous design, master the art of editing, share the wealth, and learn for yourself that gardeners do not have to dig deep to grow a lively, rich, and colorful year-round garden.

HOW PLANTS GROW

Although a wild world of variety occurs within the plant kingdom, most plants live and die by a few general rules. Use these lifecycle categories to help identify, accommodate, propagate, and manage the growth of the best plants for your garden:

- **Annuals** go through their entire lifecycle of growing, flowering, setting seed, and dying in a single season.
- **Biennials** spend one season growing roots and foliage. During their second season they flower, set seed, and die.
- **Perennials** cycle through growth, flowering, seed setting, and either stasis or full dormancy, annually, sometimes for many, many years. During dormancy —which usually occurs when light levels and/or temperatures decrease toward winter—plants may die back to the ground, sending up fresh growth the following growing season.

- **Shrubs** and **trees** go through the same yearly cycle as perennials but usually live longer. Shrubs retain a woody, multi-stemmed or low-branching structure, while trees branch higher from a single trunk. Shrubs and trees may be deciduous or evergreen during dormancy.

Plants in each lifecycle category are adapted to survive their native habitat's weather extremes, and to follow its seasonal cues to optimize growth and reproduction. (Hybrids and cultivars generally follow in the cultural footsteps of their parent species.) And quite a few—more than we could ever hope to possess—are amazingly easy to accommodate. Given a close approximation of the soil fertility and drainage, light, and climate conditions they require, they thrive.

Reproduction

When it comes right down to it, plants want to live—regardless of whether they're growing as their ancestors did on their home ground, or in your garden. They are heavily invested in the survival of their own species and they have some very clever ways to ensure generations of success.

For starters, sex sells. (Any gardener who has fallen in love—or lust—with a particular flower knows that.) DNA-laden pollen must be transferred from

LEFT Rather than let this scented geranium (*Pelargonium* 'Lady Plymouth') die outside during cold New England winters, I keep it alive in my living room.

ATTRACTING POLLINATORS

In addition to making possible new generations of showy self-sown volunteers and surprising hybrid variations, pollinators enliven the garden and give us a close personal view of nature at work. You can put out the welcome mat by refusing pesticides and by planting pollen-heavy and nectar-rich flowers like poppies, sea holly, mountain mint, and dahlias.

Pollinators also need water and places to live. A birdbath, plant saucer, or small fountain will do if you don't have space for a frog pond. Providing habitat is as easy as allowing bumblebees to nest under plants or leaf litter near a sheltering wall (while remembering to avoid that spot with your bare feet and trowel) and as cool as constructing an insect condo for several different species using found objects.

To keep butterflies in the garden, make sure their caterpillars have something to eat. Monarch butterfly caterpillars only feed on milkweed family plants (Apocynaceae) while swallowtail butterfly caterpillars prefer plants in the parsley or carrot family (Apiaceae). Send out an invitation to humming-birds by filling a feeder with diluted simple syrup (four parts water, boiled to dissolve one part sugar). Hang the feeder near a patch of their favorite flowers and replace the liquid every two or three days to prevent fermentation. You can quit filling the feeder when the birds find the flowers and have added your garden to their daily rounds.

Hollow bamboo tubes, drilled wood, piles of pottery shards, and tangles of grass and fiber offer habitat to a variety of beneficial insect and pollinator species. If you build it, they will come.

anther to stigma, one blossom to another, and in many cases, from one parent plant to another in order to keep the gene pool viable and healthy. So showy flowers are specifically engineered to seduce whichever pollinators can help them get it on. They offer their assistants gifts of high-caloric nectar and surplus nutrient-rich pollen in exchange for promiscuity.

After being fertilized by pollen dusted on a stigma and transported down the style, the flower's ovule becomes a seed. Like flowers, seeds are also designed to take advantage of the conditions in their native ecosystem. They will drop like stones, scatter, blow, be carried away, or eaten (and shat back out) depending on whatever method is most likely to result in a seedling with a good chance for survival.

If sexual reproduction ever fails, some plants fall back on asexual means of populating the earth. Plants are capable of generating clones because they are as hormonal and susceptible to influence as teenagers. The rapidly dividing cells within the leaf nodes (the point of attachment along the stem) of growing tips are especially full of growth regulators that stimulate the plant to make constant adjustments to light levels and gravity, and determine whether those versatile cells should grow into roots and a new plant, instead of leaves.

Also, when genetics place restrictions on vertical growth, allowances are sometimes made for horizontal growth. Plants then use their competitive energy to increase ranks sideways by creeping outward in ever-enlarging clumps, sending up suckers, flinging stolons in all directions, and by a slightly stealthier rhizomatous march. From our perspective as gardeners, the ways plants advance through—and over—the soil look very similar. A cheat sheet helps to recall their differences:

Honeybees and syrphid flies work a peony-flowering opium poppy (*Papaver somniferum*).

- **Suckers** are new plants that arise from a horizontal root. This is a particularly common self-propagation method for colonizing trees and shrubs.
- **Stolons or runners** are horizontal aboveground stems capable of forming adventitious roots (meaning any roots that form elsewhere than the plant's actual root system) and new plants or "plantlets" at the tips and nodes. Picture strawberries.
- **Rhizomes** are underground stems, which often look more like roots, capable of sprouting new plants. Pieces of rhizomes broken off the parent plant are usually also sufficiently hormonal to become new plants.

OPPORTUNISTIC OR INVASIVE?

Many plants walk a fine line between opportunistic and invasive. And nothing makes a gardener more nervous than a plant with exuberant growth habits or the tendency to color outside of the lines. It's perfectly natural—necessary even—for us to be a little terrified of "weeds." But not all aggressive or weedy plants are invasive. And not all invasive plants are invasive everywhere. A plant that is invasive, or potentially so, in one climate zone or ecoregion may not be invasive in another place less culturally or climatically hospitable to its needs.

The term "invasive" should be reserved for introduced species that have escaped cultivation, colonized disturbed areas and vulnerable ecosystems, outcompeted native species for local resources, or shown marked potential for any of the above. The most insidious invasives destroy habitat not only by taking over wild areas but by having inedible chemistry, depriving

LEFT Lamb's ear (*Stachys byzantina*), Mexican evening primrose (*Oenothera speciosa*), and sedums ramble opportunistically but compatibly together through this tiny dooryard garden. RIGHT A row of honesty (*Lunaria annua*) lines my fence. Its proclivity to reproduce by seed has earned it a bad rap.

native insects, and consequently the rest of the food chain—our favorite songbirds and other wildlife—with the energy they need for survival. Invasive species are a bad, bad thing. But I cry foul whenever a plant that is easy to control within a tended garden is called invasive. We can enjoy rambunctious plants while maintaining an intolerance and healthy fear of the truly invasive ones.

The hardest part is learning how to tell the difference. Although our own eyes and instincts may be relied upon the more we learn, local university extensions, Master Gardener programs, botanical gardens, and plant society chapters are our gardens' best watchdogs. We might notice that one of our plants has hopped the fence but these local authorities will know if the same plant has a habit of going even further.

The internet is a tremendous resource but beware opinions disguised as facts. Perfectly lovely plants are routinely maligned as invasive, and it can be difficult to determine what information might apply in our own neighborhood. Trust the Invasive Plant Atlas of the United States (www.invasiveplantatlas.org), which provides plant descriptions, photographs, distribution maps, and links to further information on their website. Visit www.invasive.org/species.cfm to browse invasive species lists by state. Search the United States Department of Agriculture Plant Database (www.plants.usda.gov) by plants' common or Latin names to view their native status (indicated by an N for native or I for introduced) and distribution. The Global Invasive Species Database (www.issg.org/database/welcome/) gathers and disseminates information on the world's invasive species.

We all have a responsibility to garden conscientiously, so do some research before planting anything you suspect might be invasive in your area. Take extra care if your garden is in a rural area near woods, shoreline, pasture, prairie, meadow, or mountaintop. Seeds from these gardens won't have to travel as far to disturb sensitive ecosystems so focus selections on your colorful palette of native plants, species with politely colonizing root systems, and plants with seeds that drop like stones—rather than those that fly off with the breeze or the birds. (Seeds encased in berries will be eaten and widely distributed.) Gardeners in urban or suburban areas may be allowed to live a little more dangerously. Our main responsibilities are also to resist planting nonnative species that produce seeds inside berries that birds eat, and to keep an eye on any plants that might sneak over the property line.

LEFT Oxeye daisies (*Leucanthemum vulgare*), perennial volunteers, are listed as invasive in nearly half of the United States but are manageable in my garden. Their seeds drop, and because they bloom their second year, I have months before they flower to decide what clumps to keep. RIGHT Cardoon (*Cynara cardunculus*) seeds beginning to blow away.

MAKING THE MOST OF YOUR GARDEN

Your garden should never be more expensive than you can afford or more work than you can handle. But it *could* be a colorful collage, richly patterned with drifts and repeats, different every year, and endlessly fascinating. When you allow Nature herself to take an active role in your garden's design, you can look forward to the surprises that arise. But also remember that you're under no obligation to leave plants where they land. I enjoy full editorial control. Whenever the mint encroaches on the strawberries, I unzip whole strips of their runners and ask my bartender for a mojito. Also, by following nature's lead and propagating your own plants, you'll have enough to pay it forward—and back—to friends, while keeping plenty for cohesion in your own garden (repetition being a design rule worth following).

The best place to start is by choosing plants that, once established, will thrive in your garden's particular environment without demanding supplemental watering, fertilizers, or pesticides. (Potted plants, of course, will need extra TLC.) Allow yourself to make mistakes—plants do sometimes die—but take heart that decisions become easier the better you learn how and what your garden grows. Use the hardiness, light, and soil recommendations included in the plant descriptions as skeleton keys to unlock optimal plant health and beauty.

Hardiness

The USDA plant hardiness zones (based on average annual minimum winter temperatures) are helpful indicators of which perennials, shrubs, and trees are most likely to survive our garden's wildest winter temperature dips. You can also use them to determine exactly how much protection your favorite non-hardy plants will require. Just remember that these recommendations should serve only as a guide: don't be afraid to push the zone. See "Plant Hardiness Zones" for more information, including links to interactive maps.

Light

Plants' outdoor light requirements are based on mid-summer levels, when the sun is high and hot in the sky. "Full sun" is the designation for plants that promise to grow strong and sturdy, and bloom heavily when given 6 hours or more of midday summer sun. Plants with foliage that is liable to scorch under the same conditions might need the protective cover of "full shade," even during the morning and late afternoon. Many others grow well in "partial shade"—the happy medium that ranges amenably from the dapple under a tree, to morning or late afternoon sun.

Soil

Even though soil fertility and texture varies from region to region, garden to garden, and bed to bed, the soil requirements listed in the plant descriptions are deliberately uncomplicated. Garden beds that have been amended periodically with organic matter will be perfectly adequate for most common garden plants. "Average" soil is exactly that: neither extremely fertile nor starved; neither very wet nor bone-dry. "Well-drained" soil does not puddle after rain for much more than a few minutes, while the particles of "moist" soil are capable of retaining water for days at a time without ever being boggy (that would be "wet"). "Dry" soil drains well and dries out quickly either due to sun exposure or root competition. It's safe to assume that plants requiring "rich" soil will be heavy feeders. Offer them supplemental nutrition (compost or fertilizer) especially if they are planted in a container. Reserve your lean and mean sandy soils for plants that thrive in "poor" soil and do not bother with fertilization.

For deeper insight into what your garden is capable of growing—and what changes might be necessary to grow the plants you desperately want—have your soil tested. Local university extensions and some Master Gardener programs offer soil testing and advice for a small fee.

Spacing

Because annuals and perennials are deceptively tiny in the spring, a common mistake is cramming them into beds that are too skinny to contain them as they grow. I think this is exactly why self-sowers and spreaders get a bad reputation. Plants do not need to behave themselves; the garden just needs to be more accommodating. You can avoid the frustration of hostile takeovers, and the disappointment of seeing favorites obliterated, by widening your borders—about 8 feet is a good start—so that full-grown layers of annuals, self-sowers, frost-tender and hardy perennials, and even a shrub or two, can grow comfortably together.

CONTINUE TO OBSERVE your garden as it grows and becomes transformed, and make choices considerate both to yourself and the environment. Evict any plants that cause excessive worry or trouble and try others (throw the surplus on the compost to eventually

A riot of late-summer color in Blithewold's Pollinator Garden.

COMPOST HAPPENS

Gardening with self-sowers, spreaders, and keepers is reductive—ultimately, you'll remove more than you'll plant—which is perfect for building a free and endless supply of nutrient-rich organic matter to use for replenishing depleted garden soil. The kind of compost system that you choose (enclosed tumblers or a series of open-air piles) will depend on your particular needs and garden space. Regardless, select a site for your compost area that is out of plain sight, not too far from the kitchen, easy to access with a wheelbarrow, reachable by hose, and in a somewhat sunny location.

By using enclosed bins that spin or tumble garden waste inside, it's possible to make batches of "black gold" in as little as one to three months. Tumbling composters don't hold very much fresh debris but what they lack in size, they make up for in compact good looks and relatively easy aeration. They also retain moisture well and are pest-proof.

Open-air piles take up more garden space. But, they hold a lot of debris, and if the piles are turned—aerated—weekly (use a pitchfork and don't bother buying a gym membership) they may stay hot enough to break down as quickly as in a tumbler. If you're willing to wait, piles that are turned less frequently can take up to eighteen months to produce a supply of finished compost.

Set up at least two tumblers, or make space for three open-air sections each no larger than 5 × 5 feet for manageability. Designate one tumbler or section for "cooking" or decomposing debris, another for adding fresh garden waste. Finished compost, extracted from the tumblers or the bottom of the oldest piles during turning, may be added directly back into the garden or held in the third section.

To speed the process using either system, chop everything finely before adding it to your tumbler or pile. And be careful with your ratios: thirty parts carbon (the brown bits such as dried leaves, stalks, sawdust, and shredded paper) to one part nitrogen (the green bits like plants, weeds, kitchen scraps, and grass clippings). Keep it as moist as a damp sponge and turn it often to make sure it stays hot (anywhere from 100 to 160 degrees F). One or two perforated PVC pipes inserted vertically into open-air piles will help to aerate and saturate the interior.

My open-air compost area. It's not pretty and the add-to pile is awfully high in the spring, but the pile shrinks quickly (there's always room for more) on its way to becoming my garden's best soil amendment.

Wide beds offer space for self-sowers like Mexican feather grass (*Stipa tenuissima*), sweet William catchfly (*Silene armeria*), butterfly weed (*Asclepias tuberosa*), and California poppies (*Eschscholzia californica*) to ramble alongside spreaders like Roman chamomile (*Chamaemelum nobile*), mountain mint (*Pycnanthemum muticum*), and betony (*Stachys officinalis* 'Hummelo').

become your garden's best soil amendment). The possibilities are endlessly fascinating and the potential to not just do-no-harm but to actually improve the quality and diversity of life in your garden is really, really exciting.

These are, in fact, the same negotiations with nature that most gardeners learn to make over the course of years and lifetimes. But you do not have to learn everything the hard way. Use the tools and ideas in this book to jumpstart your confidence. As soon as you begin to make adventurous decisions and exciting changes, your garden will be instantly gratifying, personally enriching, and more fun day by day, and season after season.

SELF-SOWERS

~

THE PRICE IS RIGHT

Self-sown annuals, biennials, and perennials won't come back like every other hardy plant in your garden. They're much more likely to surprise you by returning as volunteers in new places and even occasionally in different colors. Volunteers are the plants that make the garden dramatically different, and yet comfortingly familiar, from one year to the next. They'll keep you from working too hard or taking the garden too seriously, but at the same time, they make involvement obligatory. Because—and this is the fun part—to cut a diamond out of nature's rough, self-sowers have to be edited as ruthlessly as any freshman first draft.

When I started my first garden in my early twenties I was easily overwhelmed. I still remember the summer one nursery-grown borage (*Borago officinalis*) sowed a carpet of seedlings, as it will in almost any climate. I assumed that meant it was a noxious weed and evicted all of it with a couple swipes of the hoe. Weeks later, when it would have been blooming, I pined for its blue shooting stars in my salads and icy beverages. I needn't have been so hasty. Sure, some

LEFT Volunteers have been encouraged and used to their best advantage in this whimsical gravel garden. RIGHT Borage (*Borago officinalis*) flowers are edible—so pretty frozen in ice cubes—and self-sow like mad. PREVIOUS SPREAD There's no such thing as too many when self-sowers are artfully edited or as elegantly employed as these chives (*Allium schoenoprasum*) lining an herb garden path in early summer.

LEFT An artistic self-sown combination of butterfly weed (*Asclepias tuberosa*), Mexican feather grass (*Stipa tenuissima*), and betony (*Stachys officinalis* 'Hummelo'). ABOVE White corydalis (*Corydalis ochroleuca*) growing out of a rock wall at Avant Gardens in Dartmouth, Massachusetts.

plants self-sow like crazy, but they are only weeds if they grow where we don't want them. The more time I spent in my own garden with excellent plants, and in other gardens working alongside fearless mentors, the more I learned to appreciate volunteers and understand their role.

We should rely on self-sowers not just because they're free, but because they provide free labor. They plant themselves. No need to walk around the garden to find the best place for a plant. No need to dig a hole. They usually take hold where they'll thrive on benign neglect and grow into sturdy, robust plants without the coddling required of transplants. Besides being cheapest landscape crew you'll ever hire, volunteers are also the most creative. They find the places our trowels could never penetrate—like pavement cracks, stone wall pockets, and rocky crannies—and they form sublime combinations that even the trained artist in me never considers. I wish I could claim credit for planting bright orange butterfly weed against a clump of purple betony, but my design assistant, the wind, thought of that.

One-hundred-year-old trees and decades-old shrubs aren't the only plants that give a garden gravitas. Corydalis poked into nooks and growing out of crevices helps a new garden feel established—and does so much more quickly than even the fastest growing trees. Allow violets to take hold of peripheral gaps, neglected corners, tree root notches, the shady base of rock outcrops, and watch purple lovegrass (*Eragrostis spectabilis*) tuck itself into driveway cracks and ledges. Every plant that grows where a weed otherwise might, helps knit a young garden to its bones.

Self-sowers will also remind you that the garden is not a flat stage set or picture-perfect painting. It's a three-dimensional shape shifter and we rarely view any part of it exclusively from front and center. Some of us watch it from a second-story bathtub; others catch it at an oblique angle when we get into the car. I sometimes gaze at mine from ground level just for kicks. Shifts in vantage and perception give us all sorts of peeks into the garden, over and through the plants. Allow a curtain of false Queen Anne's lace (*Ammi majus*) to fall in front of an anise hyssop (*Agastache foeniculum*) for a glimpse of twilight blue through the veil. Or watch as flower-of-an-hour (*Hibiscus trionum*) weaves itself almost invisibly through the garden to decorate other plants with its surprising flowers.

Just because volunteers are free spirits (and some are downright scrappy and streetwise) doesn't mean they can't enrich a formal or modern garden with sophisticated simplicity. In fact, formality only takes a few crisp lines. And any garden with repeating textural patterns and diagonals will feel like modern art. Loose grids of blue fescue (*Festuca glauca*) or Mexican feather grass (*Stipa tenuissima*) inside knot garden parterre quadrants contrast elegantly with any clipped hedge. Cardoon carvings and teasel towers (*Cynara cardunculus* and *Dipsacus fullonum*) may stand in for expensive urns and tuteurs as architectural focal points that direct viewers' attention like a pointed finger. A garden with actual urns and tuteurs will look elegant no matter what seeds in around them.

For four-season gardens, allow plants with sturdy upright posture like anise hyssop (*Agastache foeniculum*), sculptural seedpods like honesty (*Lunaria annua*), and seedheads like dotted mint (*Monarda punctata*) and sea holly (*Eryngium planum*) to punctuate every season but spring, which doesn't need help exclaiming anyway. Let them stand through the winter, at least until the birds have had their fill of seeds or they self-destruct under the weight of the weather. Then think spring with columbine, poppies, and lupine.

A stunning woodland garden spring combo of Canada columbine (*Aquilegia canadensis*) and *Rhododendron* 'Roxanne Hardgrove'.

GUIDE TO SERENDIPITY
TAKING EDITORIAL CONTROL

t can be hard to get used to letting the wind blow and the garden grow. When self-sowers, which have little regard for group-picture rules, plant themselves where they're likely to thrive, you might find a 4-foot-tall flowering tobacco growing in the front row with the impatiens or at the very edge of a walkway. But that doesn't mean it has to stay there. Even in loosely designed naturalistic gardens we will want to preserve certain views and keep paths open and welcoming. Gardeners can encourage rowdy creativity while still taking disciplinary action when and wherever necessary. We are in charge. Move seedlings where you wish while they're young, and pluck out mature plants that have grown in the way: easy come, easy go. We might also allow a few to stand out here and there in unexpected places for the sake of spontaneous and uncontrived informality.

Seedlings that come up in the garden give us a unique opportunity to make design decisions *after* seeing what works and what doesn't. We are released from the pre-planting obligation of visualizing all of the variables that make placement a puzzle (such as where they will receive the light, water, and soil fertility they require, and look their best in combination with other plants) because as volunteers, they plant themselves. I let some of them grow long enough to see if I approve. If a plant doesn't contribute to the beauty of a view, or if it has happened to land where the chance of a healthy maturity is low, I move or remove it.

In the meantime, before decisions need to be made, it's worth letting thickly sown carpets of seedlings function as weed-defying groundcovers. Bronze fennel (*Foeniculum vulgare* 'Purpureum') and forget-me-not (*Myosotis sylvatica*) each create a fog-like layer in May that may be encouraged to float through beds before the fennel lifts skyward and the forget-me-not goes to seed. Allow deep burgundy shiso (*Perilla frutescens* var. *crispa*) seedlings to roll a red carpet under the roses or alongside sage in the herb garden. Cut the seedlings back as they grow to prolong the illusion, or pluck them out, leaving some standing in strategic spots for next year. Biennial seedlings like common teasel (*Dipsacus fullonum*) which won't flower until its second season, may function as a groundcover for the entire first season. As the garden fills in and makes their barrier less necessary, remove

---

An old wicker chair woven with *Geranium psilostemon* 'Ann Folkard' rises through a spring haze of bronze fennel (*Foeniculum vulgare* 'Purpureum') and forget-me-not (*Myosotis sylvatica*).

ABOVE LEFT Common teasel (*Dipsacus fullonum*) seedlings may be left as a weed barrier until you're ready to plant something else in their spot. They'll send up flowers the following year. ABOVE RIGHT After editing, only a few teasel are left to bloom this year.

any plants whose flowers won't be required for next year's design.

Here it must be acknowledged that most gardeners are sentimental plant lovers who find it almost impossible to throw anything healthy and attractive on the compost heap—even when facing more than we and the pollinators could possibly want. But when it comes to weeds, we're coldhearted killers. Whenever I have trouble letting go, I remind myself that weeds and self-sowers have a lot in common when they are in the wrong place. Rather than letting unwanted plants spoil your opinion of any species that's perfectly lovely in small doses, choose to be the best editor your garden has ever had. If you're ever unsure whether a volunteer should stay or go, stand back, close one eye,

and hold your thumb out over the plant in limbo like an artist critiquing a composition. If you liked the view better with it, it stays. If not, out it comes.

The soft-hearted option of transplanting seedlings instead of composting them is available when they are still young. Use your imagination to predict where you won't want them to grow and then exercise your creative muscles by designing them into different beds or combinations instead. Or donate some to friends and plant sales. The smaller they are, even if they're taprooted or resentful of disturbance, the more likely they will be to survive the move and thrive in their new digs.

To transplant whole patches of seedlings, slide a trowel or spade deeply underneath, capturing plenty of soil with the roots and taking care to keep their root systems as intact as possible. Then pot them up to give away or replant immediately. After relocation, keep seedlings watered while they become established as if you had paid top dollar at the nursery. Thin them if necessary once they have taken hold, either by cutting some off at the ground or by pulling some out (if you can do so without unearthing the whole bunch).

Besides transplanting, another excellent way to get a self-sower established in a different part of the garden is to collect and scatter its seeds, or lay a ripening seedhead down on a new patch of ground, and cross your fingers for its debut in that spot next year.

Laying the groundwork for seeds

Mulching the garden suppresses weeds, conserves moisture, and insulates root systems over the winter. Certain types of mulch also add organic matter to the soil. But when we garden with volunteers (which requires a leap of faith that seeds will, in fact, germinate), success often hinges on providing a good patch of soil for them to land on—that means go easy on the mulch.

An alternative to mulching heavily for weed suppression and moisture conservation, is to grow more plants. A chock-a-block garden and an attentive gardener will be much prettier and do a better job than any mulch in keeping weeds from taking over. Also, the more plants you have shading the bare bits (provided it's not a maple tree or willow) the more moisture retentive the soil will be.

But the happy medium in any garden, intensively planted or not, is a fine-textured mulch that covers the soil without smothering it. A condo-dwelling friend once lamented that forget-me-not refused to take hold in her foundation bed, which was buried at the condo board's insistence under 2 inches of bark mulch. Most seeds have a hard time finding traction in that stuff and it is toxic to some seedlings. But I've seen plenty of volunteers wend their way up through shredded leaves, pine needles, buckwheat hulls, and pea stone.

Sweet William catchfly (*Silene armeria*) on the move; unplanted from where it wasn't wanted, on its way to where it's needed.

Seeds just have to be able to locate some soil under the mulch and see a little light too.

Fall is a good time to apply mulch and/or compost to suppress weeds that would otherwise sprout during a warm spell, add organic matter to the soil, and provide insulation to protect shallow-rooted plants from frost heaving. Biennial seedlings will have already germinated, so make sure you don't carpet over them.

Annual seeds will be fine tucked under a light layer of mulch for the winter and will find their own way out come spring. If you use a heavy mulch as a protective winter blanket, pull it off the beds in the spring to allow the soil to warm (insulation slows heat transfer in both directions) and give your favorite volunteers a chance to germinate.

Help conserve soil moisture during the summer by spreading another light layer of mulch over exposed soil in early summer after the self-sowers have emerged and you have finished planting. Resist the urge to disturb the soil around your favorite volunteers and, as insurance, save some of their seeds to start yourself.

Forget-me-not (*Myosotis sylvatica*) seedlings germinate through buckwheat hull mulch, which is lightweight and elegant—but expensive.

Thorough deadheading of flowers before they set seed may prolong the bloom time for some plants (as well as prevent unwanted self-sowing), but it will deprive you of an even more gratifying and optimistic task: obsessive seed collection. I fill my pockets at the end of the season if only to reassure myself that spring will come again. I find it hard to quit even when my pockets overflow. But I'm always glad to have plenty of extra seeds for winter seed swaps with friends.

How will you know when a seed is ripe for saving? Every plant has its own timing, and seeds are at least as varied as dog breeds, but rattling and release are two obvious clues. Look for ripening seed capsules, which usually change color, crisping up just before opening to reveal or eject the goods inside. Opium poppies (*Papaver somniferum*), for instance, go brown from stalk to seedhead, begin to rattle, and then open vents just under their rickrack cap. Tip bunches of poppy pods upside down into paper bags to collect the countless seeds. Milkweed (*Asclepias*) pods echo fall colors and begin to split just as the seeds inside ripen. Collect the russet-brown disks when they can

Sharing seeds—the careful handoff.

be easily popped into a packet before their parachutes open and the wind catches them.

Always collect seeds on a dry day and remember to label them with name and date. Coin envelopes are the traditional seed collection containers. You can purchase boxes of five hundred (that's plenty for a season or two) and a good ten or twenty fit comfortably in a back pocket. They keep seeds dry, unless dropped in the birdbath, and are easy to write on. Small tins, spice jars, glassine stamp packets, and paper bags also work well. Resealable plastic bags are fine too as long as moisture isn't trapped in the seed.

Organized seed savers store their seed collections in shoeboxes or cookie tins with a packet of silica desiccant and a spreadsheet detailing target sow-by dates. The rest of us keep packets of seeds on the dresser, by the washing machine, and in the kitchen junk drawer; we forget to sow them on time and are grateful when nature takes its course. The cookie tin method is great because you can store it where it will be subjected to temperature fluctuations (in the refrigerator if there's room, or outside over the winter) which might help trick the seeds into germinating whenever we decide to sow them.

LEFT Butterfly weed (*Asclepias tuberosa*) seedpods beginning to open. ABOVE Rather than labeling the outside of your seed tins, write the name and date on a slip of paper and throw it in with the seeds.

HEIRLOOMS, HYBRIDS, AND SEEDLESS GREATS

Thanks to nature and plant breeders, we can count on a sliding scale of predictability when it comes to the outward appearance of self-sowers. At the most predictable end are heirlooms: carefully selected open-pollinated plants that have been sowed and saved for at least half a century Although pollinating insects, birds, and wind are in control of open-pollinated plants, they will continue to look the same from one year to the next (aside from naturally occurring mutations) as long as different species haven't been planted in close proximity. Or if we gardeners consciously choose to save seeds from the best plants and the showiest flowers, as is the case with heirlooms, our plants will actually improve over time.

Hybrids are somewhat less predictable. When wildlife and wind cross-pollinate different varieties of the same species of open-pollinated plants grow-ing in close proximity, they create a new generation that is similar but slightly different from each parent plant. If you have two different varieties of flower-ing tobacco (*Nicotiana*) in your garden, the seeds from either could become a whole new variety—a hybrid—with either a fabulous or a strangely muddy mix of characteristics. Dominant and recessive gene variations, as well as naturally occurring mutations will always present surprises, good and bad. Some-times it's best to start all over again with the strain you prefer.

F1 hybrids, on the other hand, are bred by controlled cross-pollinating of two parent species with differing traits to achieve a particular union of extra-special characteristics. They have to be created over again each season from the same parent species. With flowers, breeders are usually trying to create a new color, better height, improved sturdiness, or longer bloom time. As awesome as F1

hybrids usually are, their seeds will either be sterile or their seedlings will revert back to a disappointing parental form.

Breeders have a few excellent reasons to deliberately develop sterile or seedless plants for gardeners too. One is to create non-invasive forms of those ornamental invasive species that we all love, like purple loosestrife and butterfly bush, by making them incapable of producing healthy, viable seeds. Those plants may still spread from the roots, but at least they won't send seedlings far and wide as well. Another reason is to save gardeners the trouble of deadheading to prolong a plant's bloom time. Usually, a plant that cannot set seed will continue to bloom its head off until seasonal cues, like low daylight or cold temperatures, tell it to quit. And occasionally seed production is sacrificed when the plant's energy is spent on bigger flowers or extra petals instead. The only way for gardeners to propagate a plant that cannot self-sow is to take cuttings or divide it at the roots.

A fabulous russet sport in a patch of *Nicotiana* 'Lime Green'.

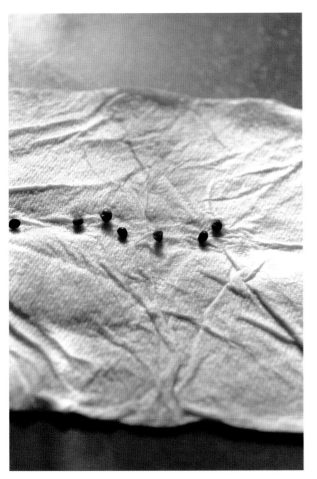

Most hardy annual and perennial seeds ripen in the summer or fall and may be stored—dry, dark, and cool—for at least one season to keep them dormant until you decide to flick the switch. Seeds that ripen in the spring should be sown immediately after collection rather than saved for later because in order to germinate they are likely to need summer's heat before winter's chill. And because the seeds of most biennials will germinate as soon as they hit the ground, in order to give their seedlings a full season to grow before flowering the next, they should also be sown as soon as possible.

A seed's lifespan also varies by species. Some will remain capable of germinating for years while others only survive dormancy for a season or two. To test whether old seeds are still viable, fold ten or so into a dampened paper towel placed inside a resealable plastic bag to keep the seeds moist, and place them where they will stay warm (about 70 degrees F), such as on top of the refrigerator. Check for sprouts after a week or two. If all seeds sprout, you win; if only one or two sprout, the germination rate will be low for the whole batch. Use your results to sow more (or less) seeds than you think you'll ultimately need.

Testing the viability of lupine seeds—only one sprouted.

PROPAGATION: SOW IT GROWS

The reason to sow seeds ourselves is to take control. We might want a say in where a plant spends its summer. We might be afraid that over the course of a season we've gardened the seeds right out of the soil. Or we might want the reassurance of having extras to tuck in and give away. Sometimes I just want to try something new. And for those of us who lack confidence, it must be admitted that successful germination is one of those little thrills worth sowing for.

Seeds are designed to take advantage of whatever conditions will guarantee germination and survival. They read light levels, soil and air temperatures, and soil pH. They are ready to germinate only when the time and place read right, which explains why some plants behave like weeds in our gardens and others come up few and far between. We can be absolutely certain that embryos need moisture in order to germinate. Another rule of thumb (whatever color you consider yours to be) is that seeds should be sown as deep as they are long. You can sprinkle really tiny

LEFT A well-outfitted seed-starting station. RIGHT
Last year's stinking hellebore (*Helleborus foetidus*) seeds
germinate alongside this season's flowers in early spring.

seeds right on the surface because the likelihood is they need light, as well as moisture, to germinate.

It gets slightly more complicated when seeds are covered in a tough coat. Those seeds may be programed to wait out a dry season, germinating only after a soaking rain; they might need to be tumbled through the gut of an animal; or they might need a cycle of freezes and thaws to soften the coat. Whichever way they work, and sometimes we have to guess, gardeners can help trigger germination by scarifying or stratifying seeds before sowing.

Scarification

Seeds from self-sowers that are native to warm zones with dry winters may need to be scarified before they'll germinate. Scarification is the process of opening a hard seed coat just enough to allow moisture in and enable the embryo to push through. You can scarify seeds by scratching the seed coat with a rasp, file, or sandpaper; nicking it with snips; or soaking it in warm water for a day until the coat softens. Be a scientist and experiment to find which method works best for your seeds. Sow scarified seeds directly in the spring garden after the last frost, or inside in dampened seed starter potting mix (more about that in "Indoor seed sowing")—either way, be sure to keep seeds moist through germination.

Stratification

Seeds from self-sowers that are native to areas with cold, snowy winters usually need to be chilled before they'll germinate. Stratification is the process of breaking dormancy by exposing seeds to moisture and wintery temperatures. Gardeners can experiment with a variety of methods, using either fake or real winter conditions.

Into the fridge or out to the shed

To stratify using your refrigerator, sandwich seeds between the folds of a damp paper towel, or within a handful of moist (not soggy) vermiculite, sand,

Seeds tacked up in the shed over the winter for stratification

or finely sifted potting mix. Place them in a resealable plastic bag in the vegetable drawer for at least a month. To really fake them out, take the seeds out of the fridge for a week at two-week intervals, to simulate freeze and thaw cycles. Or, place prepared seeds in a shed, bulkhead, or an unheated garage to go through the winter's actual temperature fluctuations.

Check on your seeds often to make sure the medium doesn't dry out, the seeds don't rot, and critters don't eat them. Gently pot them up when the seed coat has released a tiny sprout, or after a few weeks have passed even if you haven't yet seen signs of growth. If space allows, sow seeds in packs or pots instead, covered in plastic, before placing them in the cold fridge or shed. This will save you the anxiety of handling delicate sprouts after germination.

The snowmelt method

Some seeds need to be "washed" by snowmelt and any others that require winter's chill probably won't mind. If it snows in your neck of the woods you can sow seeds in a fine-textured, sterile, soilless potting mix in clean plastic pots, juice jugs, or salad boxes anytime over the winter. (The containers should be at least 2 inches deep with holes in the bottom for drainage.) Spread a thin layer of quartz pool filter sand over the top of the soil; this type of grit lets light in for the seeds that need light to germinate and holds them in place during watering. It also keeps moss from growing on moist seed starter, which is a problem especially when seeds take weeks, months, or even a year to emerge. Seed packets usually indicate how long you can expect to wait—try not to worry but recognize when to give up.

Place the containers outside and cover them securely with window screen, which will keep the wildlife out and let the snowmelt through. Protect the containers during heavy rain by bringing them inside or placing them under an overhang or garden chair. But also make sure they don't dry out.

Direct sowing

Seeds that are sown directly into the garden in fall or early spring will germinate when the time is right, no worries. Highlight the area with a thin layer of grit or sand and a label to prevent inadvertently weeding seedlings out in spring. It's also a good idea to create a blank blueprint of your garden so you can print out a new copy every year to map where you've sown what.

TOP Seeds sown in containers being washed by snowmelt.
BOTTOM Lupine seedlings germinated in April.

TIPS FOR MANAGING VOLUNTEERS AND DIRECT-SOWN SEEDLINGS

Exercise restraint. Check for signs of life around last year's patches of volunteers and your markers of winter sowings (consult your garden map if you made one). If you can't identify seedlings, wait. Give them time for their true leaves to look familiar, and if you still can't solve the mystery, wait for flowers. Likewise, if nothing has come up where you think something should, wait. The soil warms as the nights warm and some of the best self-sowers won't be triggered to germinate until early summer. Or later. If you can't wait, plant something else and cross your fingers for an interesting combination if and when survivors finally emerge.

Be your garden's best judge. I've been known to let weeds grow—just in case they might be something special—until they flower and I finally realize in a panic what they are. I don't stay embarrassed for long. Just remember, if ever you do not like the look of a plant as it grows then it probably isn't meant for your garden when it blooms either. And if you *do* like the look of a mystery plant, then it probably isn't a weed and unless it's actually invasive, don't let anyone tell you otherwise.

When necessary, commit to thin. Seedlings that come up thickly in the garden may be employed as a weed barrier at least until they start to look overcrowded. Then they should be thinned. Pull most out all at once or pull some out week by week until a precious few have the space they'll need to grow to maturity.

Get to know your seedlings. Take pictures of your most wanted self-sowers as well as your most unwanted weed seedlings as they emerge. Make a gallery to jog your own memory and put them on display for family and friends who like to help out in the garden.

Thinning self-sown love-in-a-mist (*Nigella damascena*) seedlings.

Another option is to broadcast seeds on top of the snow. This is more than just a cathartic act of optimism in the middle of winter: you can rest assured that your seeds will get any stratification and rinsing they might need as the snow melts and settles them into the soil. Tiny seeds—such as poppies, sweet alyssum (*Lobularia maritima*), love-in-a-mist (*Nigella damascena*), and larkspur (*Consolida ajacis*)—work best because they are more likely to need light to germinate once they find their way to the soil. Take care

you aim well over a patch of garden, not the lawn, and expect some shifting. Use a saltshaker to distribute seeds when mittens make it difficult to cup seeds or grasp packets.

Indoor seed sowing

Get a jump on spring by starting your seeds—whether new or saved, scarified or stratified—indoors. They'll be ready to transplant outside after they've grown big enough to handle and the weather has warmed, and will usually come into bloom weeks ahead of those directly sown outdoors. Check the Farmer's Almanac for your average last frost date and mark your calendar. Most seed packets will indicate exactly how many weeks ahead to start seeds before it's safe to plant outside. When in doubt, start seeds six to eight weeks before your average last frost.

Sow seeds in clean plastic, clay, or fiber containers in a sterile soilless seed starter or finely textured potting mix. Spread a 1/8-to 1/4-inch layer of quartz pool filter sand or chicken grit on the surface. In addition to letting in light, holding seeds in place, and hindering growth of moss, this keeps the seedlings' point of contact with the soil from being overly wet which helps prevent damping off (a common indoor seed starting fungal problem).

Water the seeds in using a watering wand or a watering can fitted with a rose that allows the water to fall gently through tiny holes, or by setting the containers in a dish of water just until the soil is evenly saturated. The latter method prevents washouts, keeps the seeds from shifting all to one side, and won't compact fine soil. Cover the containers with clear plastic to keep the soil from drying out before seeds germinate.

The biggest challenge to starting seeds indoors is providing adequate space, heat, air circulation, and light. To tease seeds into thinking it's spring, the soil they're sown in will have to be kept warm (about 70 degrees F) and moist until they hatch. The top of the refrigerator happens to be close to the ideal temperature but the lack of sufficient room up there is a drawback. So if you want to sow a lot of seeds, consider buying a heating mat, available in the spring from most hardware stores and garden centers. Regardless of location, watering with lukewarm water will also help to gently raise the soil temperature.

After germination

When the first leaves—the cotyledons—emerge, do a little dance and turn off the heat. Seedlings will grow sturdy and strong in temperatures ranging from the

Mark directly sown seeds with a wooden tag written in pencil (which doesn't fade) and a sprinkling of sand.

mid-50s F at night to the high 60s during the day. At this point seedlings also need a lot of light to keep from stretching and becoming spindly weaklings. One can only have so much south-facing windowsill space, and if yours is like mine, that sunbeam is already occupied by two cats and a dog. You're golden if you happen to have access to a greenhouse. Otherwise, hang full-spectrum fluorescent lights a few inches above the seedling tray and set the timer for sixteen to eighteen hours of light per day. Be sure to keep seedlings from drying out, but never let them sit in water once the soil is moistened through.

The plant's true leaves—you'll recognize these as tiny versions of the mature plant's leaves—will form above or alongside the cotyledons. At this point, you should begin feeding the seedlings once a week with water-soluble fertilizer diluted to half strength (there's nothing nutritious in that soilless potting mix). To prevent the air around the seedlings from stagnating, keep a fan rotating nearby at a low setting.

Culling the herd

After true leaves have formed is also the time to transplant seedlings that were sown thickly in packs or pots. Seeing seeds germinate is such a thrill that some of us may find it difficult to thin them out. But it must be done. Seeds sown thickly will compete with each other for space and nutrients and it would be tragic if none of those miracles thrived. Better to choose a few seedlings to grow on and chuck the rest.

Fill fresh pots with dampened potting mix and tamp it down to prevent air holes and settling. Use a salad fork to scoop selected seedlings from their pot and gently tease roots apart from each other. Always handle the seedlings gently by their leaves rather than their delicate stems. Then poke a root-sized hole with your finger and drop the seedling in right up to the first set of leaves (leggy stems will form roots to that point, providing a sturdier anchor) and tuck it in. Transplant only the biggest or transplant them all if you can't help yourself.

Hardening off

Seedlings sown indoors, even if they have been under lights and kept cool, will need to harden off—acclimate to living outside—before we plant them out in the garden. After night temperatures have risen reliably into the mid-50s F, place the containers outside where they'll catch morning sun for a few days before planting the seedlings in their final destination.

BELOW Seedlings under lights OPPOSITE TOP A nicotiana seedling separated from the pack. OPPOSITE BOTTOM Room to grow on.

Mexican feather grass (*Stipa tenuissima*) produces thousands of seeds.

50 FAITHFUL VOLUNTEERS

This compilation of some of my favorite volunteers is intended to plant a seed, so to speak: to inspire you to look around your friends' gardens and through seed catalogs with fresh eyes.

Pay attention to each plant's method for seed dispersal to better understand how these self-sowers should behave in your garden. Seeds that drop like stones generally germinate in the same location every season unless we inadvertently—or deliberately—transport them elsewhere. Other may be forcibly ejected, round enough to roll away, bounced out by the wind, or tossed by birds who are very messy eaters. Those scattered seeds usually do not land too far away but will manage to find surprising new territory. Seeds with wings or silk that catch on air currents also find bare ground in unexpected vacancies, but depending on the strength of the breeze, could blow into your neighbor's yard instead. I have not included plants with seeds encased in berries beloved by birds because those will end up planted miles away.

Some plants produce hundreds of seeds per flower, others just one. That along with their viability and germination rate, will affect how prolific and reliable they will be in your garden. Plants will also be more generous in some gardens than others depending on the specific conditions. Jot your own observations in the margin. Some of my favorite self-sowers are dangerously opportunistic in certain locations. Not every state has an invasive species database so if a plant you like is on a neighboring state's list, think twice before welcoming it.

This winter as you pore over your pile of seed catalogs and attend seed swaps, read and listen between the lines. Scan for words and phrases like reseeds, freely (or politely) self-sows, naturalizes, cottage garden, and old-fashioned. And notice how your garden grows more interesting and colorful with each plant you choose.

Agastache foeniculum
ANISE HYSSOP

Agastache foeniculum

Perennial | Zones 4 to 11

DESCRIPTION Midsummer through late summer, dusty-blue flower spikes—attracting every bee, hummingbird, and butterfly—top long-legged (2 to 5 ft. tall) licorice-scented stems. Allow this North American wildflower to grow in meadow-like drifts with native grasses and coneflowers, or as an architectural statement in an herb garden.

FINE PRINT Prefers full sun, and average, well-drained soil. Drought tolerant. Goldfinch and the wind help scatter the tiny seeds. Cut stems back by half in late spring for bushier growth. Deadheading encourages heavier continuous bloom, but be sure to leave some seedheads standing for winter structure.

Allium schoenoprasum
CHIVES

Allium schoenoprasum and mint growing together at the edge of a vegetable garden.

Perennial | Zones 5 to 11

DESCRIPTION Grassy tufts of 12- to 18-in. tall chives, native throughout Europe and North America, bloom in early summer with pinkish purple bundles of flowers. Traditional in vegetable beds and herb gardens, they are also excellent aphid-repelling companions for roses. Garlic chives (*A. tuberosum*, zones 4 to 8) bloom much later, toward the end of summer. Their large (2-in. wide) white star-flowered clusters become even more interesting when they shed their petals and form pepper-flake seeds cupped in beige tissue paper. Both species are entirely edible and their flowers make beautiful garnish on soup and salad.

FINE PRINT Prefers full sun, and average, well-drained soil. Seeds drop and drift. Divide large clumps of both species in early spring to keep them healthy and productive. Chives will sprout fresh leaves if entire clumps are cut to the ground after flowering.

Amaranthus cruentus
PRINCE'S FEATHER, RED AMARANTH

Amaranthus cruentus in a border at Bedrock Gardens in New Hampshire.

Annual

DESCRIPTION Cultivated across tropical regions for its grain, this plant is also a late-summer showoff in ornamental gardens (6-ft. tall beet-red plumes top stalks of red-veined green or burgundy foliage). Grow prince's feather in a cutting garden with zinnias or transplant seedlings to the back of a sunny border with nicotiana and dinnerplate dahlias. Its cousin, love-lies-bleeding (*A. caudatus*) has extremely weird, drooping cascades of ropey tassels and needs to be propped up on a fence or tied to stakes to keep them from coiling on the ground.

FINE PRINT Prefers full sun and moist soil. Seeds drop. Seedlings emerge after the soil warms and are recognizably red tinged.

Ammi majus
FALSE QUEEN ANNE'S LACE, BISHOP'S FLOWER

Ammi majus and pink peony poppy.

Annual

DESCRIPTION White cut-lace umbels (flat flower clusters) like Grandma's curtains appear atop green fretwork foliage to 4 ft. tall early in the summer and attract all sorts of bees and butterflies. Sow its romance into a rose garden, or let it form a veil around anise hyssop, sea holly, and delphinium.

FINE PRINT Prefers full sun, and rich, moist soil. Seeds drop. *A. majus* will go to seed quickly as the heat of summer hits so make sure to allow its heat-loving but less-graceful replacement, *A. visnaga* 'Green Mist', to seed itself around too—its foliage is more feathery but dense and its lace flowers are made with tighter knots.

Aquilegia
COLUMBINE, GRANNY'S BONNET

Aquilegia vulgaris 'Lime Green'

Perennial | Zones vary

DESCRIPTION There's one to decorate almost every garden from late spring to early summer. Columbine comes in all colors—even blue (*A. caerulea*, zones 4 to 7)—with and without the trademark spurs, and grow anywhere from 4 in. to 3 ft. tall from tufted rosettes of finely cut bluish foliage that persists for the whole season. Allow Canada columbine (*A. canadensis*, zones 3 to 8) with its shooting-star red and yellow blooms to sow beside golden spirea, and ask the demure double-flowered, spurless (*A. vulgaris* 'Lime Green' zones 3 to 8) or *A. chrysantha* 'Yellow Queen' (zones 3 to 9) to stand up in the front row. Different species planted near each other may cross-pollinate to create variations in color, height, and form.

FINE PRINT Prefers full sun to partial shade, and moist soil. Tiny seeds scatter when brown-bagged seedheads tip over. Columbine leaf-miner insects leave telltale trails through the leaves but do not cause fatal injury.

Asarina procumbens
CLIMBING SNAPDRAGON

Asarina procumbens

Perennial | Zones 6 to 9

DESCRIPTION I fully expect the seeds under magnification to have tiny grappling hooks and rock-climbing harnesses because they evidently love to germinate in impossible rock wall crevices and foundation cracks. Rounded furry leaves with buttercream snapdragon flowers drape and sway no more than 2 in. high and up to 24 in. long from tiny slots.

FINE PRINT Prefers full sun to partial shade, and scant amounts of well-drained soil. Tiny seeds scatter. Sow starter seeds by blowing them off the palm of your hand into crevices.

Asclepias
MILKWEED

Asclepias tuberosa

Perennial | Zones vary

DESCRIPTION The best reason to let seeds from milkweed family plants blow into the garden is because Monarch butterfly larvae feed on them exclusively. But even if they weren't an essential native host plant I would encourage butterfly weed (*A. tuberosa*, zones 4 to 9) because its brilliant 2-ft. tall orange lunar-lander flowers perfectly complement the steel blue of sea holly and make shocking combinations with hot pink sweet William catchfly and golden feverfew. Tender South American cousin, blood flower (*A. curassavica*, zones 9 to 11), doesn't return as reliably in colder zones but its two-tone, yellow-topped red flowers are wonderfully gaudy. Swamp milkweed (*A. incarnata*, zones 3 to 8) is taller at 3 to 4 ft. and eraser-pink; *A. incarnata* 'Ice Ballet' is a more genteel creamy-white.

FINE PRINT Prefers full sun and average soil. Seedpods become sunset-tinted in fall and split lengthwise before releasing their parachutes. To take control of seeding, collect the seeds right after the pods open, and direct sow in fall or early spring.

Begonia grandis
HARDY BEGONIA

Begonia grandis

Perennial | Zones 6 to 9

DESCRIPTION Translucent olive-green off-center hearts with red veins and backsides rise on 1- to 2-ft. tall red stems out of the shade garden in spring. From late summer to frost bubblegum-pink or white flowers with yellow centers open from nodding clamshell buds. Encourage hardy begonia to pick up where spring ephemerals leave off around astilbes, hostas, and ferns and it will steal the shade garden's show whenever it is backlit by the sun.

FINE PRINT Prefers partial shade to shade, and moist, slightly acidic soil. Hardy begonias self-propagate by dropping bulbils (clones) from the leaf axils as well as seeds. Transplant soon after they emerge in late spring or early summer.

Calamintha nepeta subsp. *nepeta*
CALAMINT

Calamintha nepeta subsp. *nepeta*

Perennial | Zones 4 to 9

DESCRIPTION Tufted mounds of 12- to 18-in. tall, deep green aromatic leaves are topped from midsummer on with clouds of white to pale bluish flower spires that never need deadheading. This doesn't have its mint cousins' reputation for thuggishness but in my garden it has spread both rhizomatously and by seed to form a nebulous groundcover around beach roses and kniphofia.

FINE PRINT Prefers full sun to partial shade, and average, well-drained soil. Drought tolerant. Seeds drop. Use extra seedlings and offshoots as bee-friendly fillers in containers. Cut stems to the ground in late fall or early spring.

Cleome hassleriana
SPIDER FLOWER, CAT'S WHISKERS

Cleome hassleriana

Annual

DESCRIPTION What was Grandma smoking? Cleome is a traditional back-row cottage garden plant but the foliage is suspicious looking and the flower is far out. White, pink, or purple petals, depending on variety, continuously open into oval flares from cell-tower buds and send their stamens and then tubular seedpods out like whiskers that work their way down the stalk, even as the flower rises to its full 5 ft. Allow the sticky and spiny brutes to sow themselves out of your way against a fence or hedge that displays their radical structure in silhouette.

FINE PRINT Prefers full sun and average soil. Seeds scatter as they pop out of pods. Cleome becomes robust and well-branched with water and rich soil. To stunt its growth, give it less love.

Coix lacryma-jobi
JOB'S TEARS

Coix lacryma-jobi

Annual grass

DESCRIPTION This plant might bring out the obsessive seed saver in you. Strappy corn-like grass-green blades growing 18 to 36 in. tall are interrupted at intervals by unnoticeable flowers, followed by bangles of shiny tear-shaped beads that arch outwards and turn from apple-green to brown, black, and gray. Collect them for the satisfying clack of a pocketful, to string them into bracelets, or to guarantee another generation. This slender plant is best wedged in between sturdier ones like black-eyed Susan and echinops.

FINE PRINT Prefers full sun and average soil. Seeds drop. Soak or scarify heavy beads (lightweight ones are empty) to speed the germination process when starting seeds indoors.

Consolida ajacis
LARKSPUR

Consolida ajacis

Annual

DESCRIPTION If delphinium is unreliable in your garden, try larkspur. The foliage is more finely feathery and the fully double flowers—pink, white and lavender, or deep purple-blue with long spurs that hover off the stem like butterflies—are daintier. But en masse, the delicate 1- to 3-ft. spires of poor man's delphinium make a luxurious early to midsummer show. Thin seedlings to about 3 in. apart and pair them with California poppies and apricot-colored roses.

FINE PRINT Prefers full sun, and rich, well-drained soil. Tiny seeds scatter. Larkspur is a cool-season annual that burns out in summer's heat. For a repeat show, stratify seeds for a couple of weeks in the refrigerator and start them in the cool dark. After germination, give the seedlings plenty of light before planting them to fill late summer gaps.

Corydalis ochroleuca

WHITE CORYDALIS

Corydalis ochroleuca

Evergreen perennial | Zones 6 to 8

DESCRIPTION White corydalis doesn't seem to care whether it grows out of a rock wall crevice or on a wide patch of ground but it looks best tucked by itself into a cranny. Wherever it grows it will fill its space with 12-in. tall bluish green eyelet-lace foliage and early-summer sprays of tiny tubular flowers with a flared face tinged with green and yellow. White corydalis' cousin, yellow corydalis (*C. lutea*, zones 5 to 8) blooms on and off all summer. Fern-leaf corydalis (*C. cheilanthifolia*, zones 6 to 8) might be mistaken for a fern if it weren't for its spikes of banana yellow flowers in early summer.

FINE PRINT Prefers full sun to shade, and rich, well-drained soil. Tiny seeds scatter. Saved seeds need warm and cold stratification to germinate. Transplant seedlings in spring into tree root notches and against rock outcrops.

Cynara cardunculus

CARDOON

Cynara cardunculus

Perennial | Zones 7 to 10

DESCRIPTION Cardoon is like an artichoke on steroids. Grow it for 3-ft. wide verdigris leaves that provide focal points as elegant as bronze sculptures and because the bees love to circle their 3- to 6-ft. tall purple thistle-like air traffic control towers. If left standing through fall, the flowers fade to chocolate-brown seedheads topped by downy cushions.

FINE PRINT Prefers full sun and average soil. Seeds blow. New plants and offshoots bloom their second year. Despite a deep taproot, they may be transplanted in spring. Give cardoon space to keep its arching leaves from flattening or shading out more delicate neighbors. To control reseeding, cut stalks down before seedheads self-destruct over the winter. **INVASIVE** in California.

Dicentra eximia

WILD BLEEDING HEART, FERN-LEAF BLEEDING HEART

Dicentra eximia

Perennial | Zones 3 to 8

DESCRIPTION While most bleeding hearts go dormant after their exuberant spring show, wild bleeding heart keeps on trucking. Diminutive tufts of delicately cut blue-gray leaves growing 6 to 20 in. tall are topped almost continuously by tiny heart-shaped flowers that take a rest only during the hottest weeks. Encourage this eastern United States native to self-sow through a woodland glade with creeping phlox, hostas, and true ferns.

FINE PRINT Prefers partial shade, and rich, moist soil. Ants help distribute dropped seeds which will germinate the following spring after both warm and cold periods of stratification. Seeds need light to germinate.

Digitalis purpurea

COMMON FOXGLOVE

Digitalis purpurea

Biennial or short-lived perennial | Zones 4 to 8

DESCRIPTION The presence of these open-mouthed tubular flowers in white, pink, apricot, and purple (mostly purple) arranged on one side of 3- to 6-ft. tall gracefully arching stems makes every early-summer shade combination of heuchera, hosta, and geranium much more interesting. Yellow foxglove (*D. grandiflora*, perennial, zones 3 to 8) only grows to about 3 ft. tall and returns less abundantly, but blooms longer into the summer than common foxglove.

FINE PRINT Both species prefer partial shade and average soil and are entirely poisonous unless administered by your doctor to treat heart problems. Seeds drop and need light to germinate. Sow in early spring and transplant seedlings in the fall to bloom the following summer. Purplish seedlings will have purple blooms. Common foxglove is **INVASIVE** in California, Oregon, and Washington.

Dipsacus fullonum
COMMON TEASEL

Dipsacus fullonum seedheads caught in autumn spiderwebs.

Biennial | Zones 5 to 8

DESCRIPTION In my garden, common teasel behaves beautifully, attracting bees with its 6-ft. tall towers topped by pale green barbed eggs ringed in pollen-heavy lavender flowers that open in sequence from the center up and down. I rely on their sturdy architecture long after the flowerheads and stalk turn a crispy beige, and I love watching goldfinch snag seeds.

FINE PRINT Prefers full sun to partial shade, and average soil. Seeds scatter and all that land on bare earth germinate in spring. Taprooted seedlings remain a ground-level rosette for their first season and are easy to remove by hand or hoe. Transplant small in late spring. Second-year plants become as spiny as thistle.
INVASIVE in California, Colorado, Idaho, Illinois, Kentucky, Michigan, Missouri, New Jersey, Ohio, Oregon, Tennessee, Virginia, Washington, and Wisconsin. Alternative: Canadian burnet (*Sanguisorba canadensis*).

Eragrostis spectabilis
PURPLE LOVEGRASS, TUMBLEWEED GRASS

Eragrostis spectabilis

Perennial grass | Zones 5 to 8

DESCRIPTION Bone-straight blades that fan out in all directions from a central point are separated and nearly completely hidden in late summer by a cloud of 18- to 24-in. purplish red inflorescence that catches diamond-like dew. The low-to-the-ground muffin shape of this North American grass is perhaps not as graceful as other ornamental grasses that toss in the wind, but it makes a misty complement for the solidity of fall-blooming stonecrop and asters.

FINE PRINT Prefers full sun, and poor, dry to average soil. The seedheads detach in fall and winter and blow around the garden like tiny tumbleweeds; it also spreads slowly by rhizomes. Cut blades to the ground in late winter or early spring.

Erigeron karvinskianus 'Profusion'
FLEABANE

Erigeron karvinskianus 'Profusion'

Perennial | Zones 7 to 11

DESCRIPTION Fleabane evidently loves tight confines like rock walls and pavement cracks where its profusion of dime-sized multicolored daisies (yellow-centered white fading to deep pink) make a frothing mound (8 to 12 in. tall × 2 ft. wide) that softens hard edges. Let it flow down slopes around sedum and lavender.

FINE PRINT Prefers full sun to partial midday shade, and average, well-drained soil. Seeds blow. It will happily seed itself into containers, to spill over the sides and flower on and off all winter indoors. To survive or reseed outdoors it needs sharp winter drainage. Seeds need light to germinate.

Eryngium planum
SEA HOLLY

Eryngium planum with a red admiral butterfly and betony.

Perennial | Zones 5 to 9

DESCRIPTION I have counted at least a dozen different species of bee and wasp working sea holly's cobalt blue thimbles. The flowers appear on well-branched, blue-washed, prickly stems (24 to 36 in. tall) from a basal rosette of leathery deep green leaves and turn beige from the top down as seeds ripen. Stems have weak ankles and may need to be propped against a fence, or a sturdy clump of butterfly weed or Shasta daisies (*Leucanthemum ×superbum)*.

FINE PRINT Prefers full sun, and poor to average, well-drained soil. Leave ornamental seedheads standing into fall or winter to give seeds a chance to drop and scatter. Transplant taprooted seedlings in early spring while they are still small.

Eschscholzia californica
CALIFORNIA POPPY

Eschscholzia californica dotted brightly among *Kalimeris incisa* 'Blue Star'

Annual

DESCRIPTION There's nothing as cheerful or as persistent as a poppy. Over-saturated silky orange, yellow, red, pink, or white cups that open and close with the sun, look almost too large for their delicate gray fern-leaf foliage that stretches to 12 in. Give this western wildflower the opportunity to weave itself around euphorbia and blue fescue and bloom its heart out from late spring well into summer and fall.

FINE PRINT Prefers full sun, and poor to average, well-drained soil. Tiny seeds pop out of skinny pods. Mixed colors and doubles usually come back as orange and yellow. Plants are taprooted and resentful of transplanting unless moved by careful spade-full in early spring.

Euphorbia
SPURGE

Euphorbia longifolia 'Amjilassa'

Perennials and annuals | Zones vary

DESCRIPTION At least a half dozen garden-worthy species of euphorbia (out of all two thousand) self-sow freely. Perennial *E. longifolia* 'Amjilassa' (zones 6 to 9), grows 2 ft. tall with intensely yellow flower bracts in spring and white-veined leaves. Leave clumps to rebloom (cut spent stems to the ground) or pull most out after blooming to make room for late-blooming annuals and tender perennials. Wood spurge (*E. amygdaloides* 'Purpurea', perennial, zones 6 to 9) colonizes moist shade by rhizome and seed to display 1- to 2-ft. tall cymes of acid-green avant-garde flowers in spring that bring out the best in hosta. North American native snow-on-the-mountain (*E. marginata*, annual) grows 1 to 3 ft. tall with variegated foliage and showy green and white bracts in midsummer. *E. corollata*, a native Nebraskan (perennial, zones 4 to 7), has white summer blooms that look just like baby's breath on stems up to 3 ft. tall.

FINE PRINT Prefers full sun and well-drained soil. Seeds scatter. Spurge bleeds a sticky latex that can cause angry skin rashes (wear gloves) and severe discomfort if accidentally ingested. The upside is that deer and rabbits leave it alone.

Festuca glauca
BLUE FESCUE

Festuca glauca

Perennial grass | Zones 4 to 8

DESCRIPTION Hedgehog-like clumps of 8- to 12-in. tall thin blue blades are excellent echoes for the blue-gray mounds of catmint and lavender. In late spring to early summer they are spiked with pale green flowers, then tan seedheads that give them a few more inches in height. Some gardeners do not like the look of the flowers and remove them long before they set seed; I prefer to let the flowers remain for the promise of extra plants.

FINE PRINT Prefers full sun to partial shade, and poor to average, well-drained soil. Seeds drop. After a couple of seasons in the garden, mature clumps die in the center and stop looking as cute. At that point they should be divided or replaced with a spare.

Foeniculum vulgare 'Purpureum'
BRONZE FENNEL

Foeniculum vulgare 'Purpureum'

Perennial | Zones 4 to 9

DESCRIPTION Feathery, licorice-scented, tarnished bronze foliage contrasts with almost everything. Allow seedlings to form a groundcover around spring bulbs, plant it with plume poppy for an elegant textural contrast, or let it shade the lettuce in a midsummer vegetable patch. Wherever bronze fennel grows, it will attract swallowtail butterflies—their caterpillars love it.

FINE PRINT Prefers full sun and average soil. Seeds scatter. Cut bronze fennel back by half in early summer to stunt its height and delay bloom (relocate caterpillars to lower leaves). A deep taproot makes this plant tough to remove once established so spade out unwanted seedlings before they grow taller than 2 ft. **INVASIVE** in California, Hawaii, Oregon, Virginia, and Washington. Alternative: golden Alexander (*Zizia aurea*).

Helleborus foetidus
STINKING HELLEBORE

Helleborus foetidus

Perennial | Zones 6 to 9

DESCRIPTION Pale green buds rise 2 ft. or so from beneath cloaks of deep green almost black fanned foliage. In late winter to early spring, when almost nothing else will bloom, the buds open into odd red-rimmed dangling green bells. I've never abused the leaves to see if they stink when crushed, but I've also never leaned down for a whiff of a flower, which are supposed to be pleasantly scented. Plant them as a gothic foil for hosta and heuchera.

FINE PRINT Prefers partial shade, and rich, well-drained, neutral to alkaline soil. Ants help disperse dropped seeds but most germinate the following spring right alongside the parent plants. Seedlings may be easily transplanted in spring.

Hibiscus trionum
FLOWER-OF-AN-HOUR

Hibiscus trionum

Annual or short-lived perennial | Zones 10 to 12

DESCRIPTION Flower-of-an-hour always surprises me by weaving its 12- to 30-in. tall stems almost invisibly through the garden to decorate other plants with 2-in. creamy white satellite-dish blooms with bottomless purple centers surrounding golden anthers. Get them started wherever early-summer bloomers like catmint go quiet over late summer and among foliage plants like basil that could use a flower in their ear.

FINE PRINT Prefers full sun and moist soil. Flowers only open for an hour or two while the sun is out and the temperature is warm. Yesterday's flowers become green fuzzy, darkly veined balloons before turning a crispy chocolate brown and splitting across the top to reveal and drop ripe seeds.

Lobularia maritima
SWEET ALYSSUM

Lobularia maritima

Annual

DESCRIPTION For such a tiny flower sweet alyssum packs a powerful honey scent that doesn't require a nose to the ground to detect. Grow the 4- to 8-in. tall × 12-in. wide pillows of purple, lavender, or white flowers in the vegetable garden to repel flea beetles, or at the edges of an ornamental border, along walls, and in pavement cracks.

FINE PRINT Prefers full sun, and average to moist soil. Trim flowers after the first flush to encourage rebloom but allow a few to drop seeds for a succession of seedlings capable of blooming until a killing frost.

Lunaria annua
HONESTY, MONEY PLANT

Lunaria annua coming up through a Tiger Eyes staghorn sumac.

Biennial | Zones 3 to 9

DESCRIPTION Coarse clumps of large heart-shaped leaves have a weedy look but the second-year flowers and translucent seedpods that fade from blue-green to silver are pretty enough to justify waiting out their awkward phase. The purple cruciform flowers that top its 36-in. tall stems in spring are the perfect complement to acid-green spurge and emerging Tiger Eyes staghorn sumac foliage.

FINE PRINT Prefers full sun to partial shade, and average soil. The seedpods are essential for dried flower arrangements in winter, but leave a few in the garden so seeds can drop and blow into new combinations.
INVASIVE in Oregon.

Lupinus
LUPINE

Perennial | Zones vary

DESCRIPTION Although lupines come in a full-spectrum of colors, nothing compares with the indigo blues of the East Coast's wild lupine (*L. perennis*, zones 4 to 8), Texas bluebonnet (*L. texensis*, annual), California's silver lupine (*L. albifrons*, zones 9 to 10), and the large-leaved lupine of the western United States (*L. polyphyllus*, zones 5 to 8), parent of 4-ft. tall Russell hybrids. Vertical flower spikes in early summer provide structure for poppies and spring meadow flowers, and their fanned palmate leaves display dew like mercury. Lupines also fix atmospheric nitrogen to improve poor soil.

FINE PRINT Prefers full sun to partial shade, and average, well-drained soil (*L. polyphyllus* prefers moist conditions). Seeds scatter, ejected from blackened peapods. Taproots make transplanting difficult so move seedlings young. To maintain variability in multicolored Russell hybrids remove dominant-gene-laden blue flowers prior to pollination.

A reverted *Lupinus* Russell hybrid.

Lychnis coronaria
ROSE CAMPION

Lychnis coronaria

Biennial or short-lived perennial | Zones 3 to 8

DESCRIPTION Woolly gray 2- to 3-ft. tall stems are topped with loud, super-saturated cerise pink disks—this is the kind of color that would be in poor taste if it appeared in our trouser drawer. But when rose campion seeds itself alongside lavender, red roses, orange butterfly weed, or golden feverfew it gives the garden, and any expectations we might have of cultured elegance, a terrific kick in the pants. For quiet gardens and color-shy gardeners, choose toned-down cultivars with white and paler pink flowers.

FINE PRINT Prefers full sun to partial shade, and average soil. Tiny seeds drop. First-year seedlings are easy to transplant anytime; move second-year seedlings in early spring.

Meconopsis cambrica
WELSH POPPY

Meconopsis cambrica

Perennial | Zones 6 to 10

DESCRIPTION Not everyone has the right conditions to grow Himalayan blue poppy (*Meconopsis betonicifolia*) but its Welsh cousin is much easier to please. Wrinkled yellow to orange cups dance on 18-in. stems in the slightest breeze from spring to fall. The bright flowers are also a pretty shade garden companion to hosta, lady's mantle, and heuchera.

FINE PRINT Prefers partial shade, and average to moist soil. Seeds drop and scatter when tiny flaps open at the top of torpedo-shaped pods. Beware the plant's taproot, which can rudely insert itself inside the crown of other plants and resprout if snapped. Evict squatters while they're young and easy to pluck out whole.

Monarda punctata
DOTTED MINT, SPOTTED BEEBALM

Monarda punctata

Annual or short-lived perennial | Zones 4 to 9

DESCRIPTION From a distance, dotted mint's miniature pagoda flowers are pale and textural, particularly when paired with black-eyed Susans and ornamental grasses. Up close you'll get lost in the intricacy of purplish pink bracts, tinged green at the tips, separating whorls of speckled yellow flowers. The 12- to 36-in. tall towers of these North American natives look even more exotic capped by hungry goldfinch.

FINE PRINT Prefers full sun to partial shade, and average, well-drained soil. Seeds drop and scatter. Seedlings are recognizable for downy-soft square stems and narrow leaves delicately edged and veined in hot pink. Transplant them in spring or fall.

Myosotis sylvatica
FORGET-ME-NOT

Myosotis sylvatica and a variegated Japanese sedge.

Biennial or short-lived perennial | Zones 5 to 9

DESCRIPTION In mid to late spring, tiny cerulean flowers with daffodil-yellow eyes grow 5 to 12 in. from tuffets of basal foliage and glow as if the sky itself was thrown over the garden's beds. Pair it with the late-blooming green-streaked *Tulipa* 'Artist' (or another orange tulip) and use it as a placeholder for summer annuals and tender perennials by removing entire plants after they have gone to seed.

FINE PRINT Prefers full sun to partial shade, and average soil. Seeds drop. Remove plants after blooming and disperse their seeds with a flick of the wrist. (Seeds will also stick to cuffs and fur, scattering as you and the dog travel through the garden.) Be careful to avoid weeding out all of next year's seedlings, which germinate quickly after dispersal. Seedlings can be transplanted in fall or early the following spring. **INVASIVE** in Wisconsin.

Nicotiana
FLOWERING TOBACCO

Nicotiana 'Lime Green'

Annual

DESCRIPTION White flowering fragrant *N. alata* and *N. sylvestris* have large, smothering, sticky basal leaves but delicate 5-ft. spires of white trumpets (*N. sylvestris* flowers are clustered at the tippy-top) that open to waft sweetness at night. *N. mutabilis* 'Bella' stands 3 to 4 ft. tall with multicolored flowers that fade from almost white to a rosy pink. *N. langsdorffii* also has tall stems abundantly dangled with small apple-green bells beloved by hummingbirds. *N.* 'Lime Green' has outward-facing green flowers and stands only 1 to 3 ft. tall. Plant tall species at the back of a border to come up between anise hyssop and amaranth.

FINE PRINT Prefers full sun to partial shade, and average soil. Tiny seeds drop and scatter; plants also return from the roots after mild winters. Cut stems back hard after flowering to encourage reblooming but come late summer, allow some seedheads to form. Cross-pollination produces interesting hybrids and variations.

Nigella damascena
LOVE-IN-A-MIST, DEVIL-IN-A-BUSH

Nigella damascena

Annual

DESCRIPTION Cobalt blue—or white or pink—flowers with twist-tie centers and a tangled ruff of wiry foliage are bizarre but the swollen red and green jester-capped seedpods might have been designed by Tim Burton. The 2-ft. tall plants are slender and feathery enough to fit in among daisies and roses that bloom in early summer and they positively vibrate with California or Atlantic poppies. Use the Willy Wonka seedheads to lend a bit of strangeness to floral arrangements. They dry well but lose their color.

FINE PRINT Prefers full sun, and poor to average soil. Seeds drop when the pods turn beige and split at the top. Transplant seedlings while they are young and thin them to 2 to 3 in. apart for showier blooms and pods.

Ocimum basilicum 'Blue Spice'
BLUE SPICE BASIL

Ocimum basilicum 'Blue Spice'

Annual

DESCRIPTION Some gardeners love blue spice basil for its vanilla scent and sweet flavor in fruit salads but the bees and I prefer to keep its fuzzy leaves and pale purple flowers in the garden. The small plants (12 to 18 in. tall) willingly fill in around annual grasses and dahlias and go perfectly well with beebalm, yarrow, and calendula in an herb garden.

FINE PRINT Prefers full sun to partial shade, and average soil. Seeds drop. The flowers don't need to be deadheaded to keep the plant productive—they'll keep going from midsummer to frost.

Orlaya grandiflora
WHITE LACE FLOWER, MINOAN LACE

Orlaya grandiflora with California poppies.

Annual

DESCRIPTION Tatted doilies aren't just for maiden aunts. This plant combines the featheriness of false Queen Anne's lace (without their height) and the flower structure of lace cap hydrangea (large outer petals surround small true flowers). With 18- to 24-in. tall stems, they make excellent cut flowers and add elegance to early-summer garden combinations of California poppies, sweet William catchfly, and Mexican feather grass. Frequent visitors to the flowers include bees as well as syrphid flies—terrific tiny pollinators whose larvae eat aphids.

FINE PRINT Prefers full sun and average soil. Seeds drop and scatter by attaching like Velcro to clothing and fur. Pull plants after they have gone to seed (save some first) and insert late-summer bloomers to fill their vacancies.

Papaver atlanticum

Papaver atlanticum

ATLANTIC POPPY, MOROCCAN POPPY

Short-lived perennial | Zones 5 to 7

DESCRIPTION Orange flowers have a way of making every other color in the garden sparkle. Let the wrinkled, apricot-orange flowers of Atlantic poppy shimmer delicately 12 to 24 in. above sky blue forget-me-nots. Gray-green basal rosettes, stems, and skinny seedpods begin to predominate as flowering slows down after early summer.

FINE PRINT Prefers full sun to partial shade, and average soil. Drought tolerant. Seeds drop and bounce. For continuous bloom, deadhead down to fresh buds, or yank spent stems from the base to make way for new growth. Alternatively, remove entire clumps to make room for planting new annuals and tender perennials. They resent transplanting, so move them young.

Papaver somniferum

OPIUM POPPY, PEONY POPPY

Papaver somniferum

Annual

DESCRIPTION Grow opium poppies for the one-time-only large flowers that unfold out of small nodding buds in early summer. The 4-ft. tall stems of silvery gray-green ruffled foliage bear 4-in. flowers, each one decorated dawn to dusk with bees and syrphid flies. After the flowers shatter, their ornamental seedpods may be peeled open by addicted goldfinch.

FINE PRINT Prefers full sun and average soil. Drought tolerant. Hundreds of tiny seeds drop out of open vents in browned seedpods. Seeds may live for years and pop up unexpectedly in freshly disturbed soil. Different varieties will cross-pollinate to produce mongrels and fabulous hybrids. It is illegal in the United States to "knowingly" grow opium poppies. But you didn't hear that from me.

Perilla frutescens var. *crispa*
SHISO, BEEFSTEAK PLANT

The burgundy foliage of *Perilla frutescens* var. *crispa* picks up the pink in 'Baby Bella' flowering tobacco.

Annual

DESCRIPTION It is often hard to decide what to do with an ornamental edible. Enjoy it for its looks, or pull and eat it? Shiso self-sows generously into a burgundy carpet that may be left as a weed barrier until you need the space for late-blooming annuals and tender perennials. Just leave a few to grow to maturity as a dark backdrop for spur flower and hummingbird mint. Stems grow 1 to 3 ft. tall and keep their color but the pink autumn flower spires aren't especially showy.

FINE PRINT Prefers full sun to partial shade, and moist soil. Seeds drop. Thin seedlings to use as grapefruit-flavored vitamin-rich leaves in salads and sushi or transplant them in early summer. **INVASIVE** in the District of Columbia, Illinois, Maryland, Missouri, Pennsylvania, Tennessee, Virginia, and West Virginia. Alternative: purple basil (*Ocimum basilicum*).

Salvia sclarea
CLARY SAGE

Salvia sclarea var. *turkestanica* 'Alba'

Biennial or perennial | Zones 5 to 9

DESCRIPTION Clary sage's large textured gray-green leaves are nothing compared to those of silver sage (*S. argentea*), but its flowers are spectacular. Abundant sprays of luminous pink to purple-tinged or green-tinged white flowers with wide showy bracts rise at least 3 ft. from the ground and dominate the limelight for weeks in early summer. Pair it with feathery love-in-a-mist or let this traditional medicinal self-sow in an herb garden alongside lavender and beebalm.

FINE PRINT Prefers full sun, and dry to average, well-drained soil. Seeds drop. Transplant seedlings in spring. Cut spent stems to the ground after seeds ripen and give a flick of the wrist to scatter them. **INVASIVE** in Washington.

Silene armeria
SWEET WILLIAM CATCHFLY, NONE-SO-PRETTY

Silene armeria

Perennial | Zones 5 to 8

DESCRIPTION Regardless of sweet William catchfly's usefulness as a flytrap (to me their 2-ft. tall stems feel more rubbery than sticky) I'm stuck to their intensely purplish pink pinwheel flower clusters that clash so brilliantly with chrome-yellow euphorbias, orange California poppies, red roses, and cobalt blue love-in-a-mist.

FINE PRINT Prefers full sun to light shade, and average, well-drained soil. Seeds drop. Commonly described as blooming in late summer, I have always observed its display in early to midsummer. Transplant in spring.

Stipa tenuissima

Stipa tenuissima, syn. *Nassella tenuissima*

MEXICAN FEATHER GRASS

Perennial grass | Zones 7 to 11

DESCRIPTION Tufts of the finest green-gold filaments wave in the slightest breeze like long hair underwater. Early-summer flowers add volume to its tresses, which turn blond by mid to late summer. Allow Mexican feather grass to grow wherever its movement will offer a contrast to less kinetic companions such as yarrow or spurge.

FINE PRINT Prefers full sun, and average, well-drained soil. Seeds can blow but many drop because as the seedheads dry, they tangle, mat, and weigh the clump down. Comb its "hair" with your fingers to capture seeds and open the grass back up to the wind. Where hardy, do not cut it back like other grasses in spring. Transplant seedlings any time. **INVASIVE** in California, Australia, New Zealand, and South Africa. Alternative: purple three awn (*Aristida purpurea*).

Stylophorum diphyllum

CELANDINE POPPY

Stylophorum diphyllum

Perennial | Zones 5 to 8

DESCRIPTION Celandine poppy, a native to eastern United States, should get at least partial credit for yellow being spring's color. The super-saturated sunshiny flowers, opening from fuzzy buds atop lobed gray-green foliage on 12-in. tall stems, are timed to follow the daffodils and partner with Virginia bluebell (*Mertensia virginica*), lungwort (*Pulmonaria*), and foamflower.

FINE PRINT Prefers partial shade to shade, and rich, moist soil. Seedpods nod their heads and open like bell-bottoms to drop tiny seeds dispersed by ants. Like most other spring ephemerals, celandine poppies go dormant during hot dry summers; if your woodland garden stays moist, you can trick them into an eternal spring by deadheading flowers before they go to seed.

Talinum paniculatum
JEWELS OF OPAR

Talinum paniculatum

Perennial grown as an annual | Zones 13 to 15

DESCRIPTION Succulent clusters of paddle-shaped leaves send up see-through stems dressed only in airy sprays of tiny pink afternoon flowers that turn into shiny red-purple polka-dots that hang on and turn brown only as the seeds inside ripen. Allow swaths of this southern and tropical American wildflower to form along the front of borders, transplant a few into containers, and use the stems as bobbles in flower arrangements.

FINE PRINT Prefers full sun, and dry to average, well-drained soil. Seeds drop. The cultivar 'Kingswood Gold' has bright chartreuse leaves and comes true from seed. Fleshy seedlings are easy to recognize whether they are grass-green or yellow-green. Transplant them young.

Tanacetum parthenium
FEVERFEW

Tanacetum parthenium 'Aureum'

Short-lived perennial | Zones 4 to 9

DESCRIPTION In midsummer, tiny daisies dot 18- to 24-in. tall stems with aromatic gray-green foliage; golden feverfew (*T. parthenium* 'Aureum') has yellow-green foliage. Let it self-sow into the herb garden as a salute to its medicinal properties—it is used to prevent migraine headaches and relieve arthritis pain. Or because bees avoid it, use it as a buffer along walkways and sitting areas in an otherwise bee-friendly garden.

FINE PRINT Prefers full sun to partial shade, and dry to average, well-drained soil. Tiny seeds blow. All cultivars are self-fertile, which means that crossing is unlikely. Cut plants back to encourage reblooming. Seeds need light to germinate. Transplant in spring or fall.

Verbascum

MULLEIN

A *Verbascum epixanthinum* cross.

Biennials and short-lived perennials | Zones vary

DESCRIPTION Grow purple mullein (*V. phoeniceum*, zones 4 to 8) for its 4-ft. tall spears of wide-open purple, white, or pink flowers reminiscent of delphinium and enjoy the variations that arise in late spring to early summer with each new generation. For vertical action in mid to late summer, grow Turkish mullein (*V. bombyciferum* 'Artic Summer', zones 5 to 9) which has a voluptuously woolly first-year basal rosette and 5-ft. tall spires of yellow flowers; or the 3-ft. tall nettle-leaved mullein (*V. chaixii*, zones 5 to 9), which also has felted basal leaves and second-year pale yellow flowers with purple centers. As tall as the flower towers are, placement at the front of the border with catmint and creeping Jenny will showcase their low gray rosettes.

FINE PRINT Prefers full sun, and poor, well-drained soil. Seeds drop. Flowers may need to be staked in rich soil. Keep your eyes peeled for hummingbirds who use the soft leaves to line their nests. Common mullein or Aaron's rod (*V. thapsus*) is **INVASIVE** throughout the United States.

Verbena bonariensis

TALL VERBENA, TALL VERVAIN

Verbena bonariensis

Perennial | Zones 7 to 11

DESCRIPTION I roll my eyes at abundant spring carpets of telltale purplish seedlings but I rely on them to grow into latticework screens that frame my views through beds and borders. From early summer to fall, deep purple-green virtually leafless sandpaper stems branch in wide forks topped anywhere from 3 to 5 ft. with purple butterfly landing pads. (A butterfly on a plant always improves my opinion of it.)

FINE PRINT Prefers full sun and average soil. Tiny seeds ripen and drop before flower clusters finish blooming and germinate in endless succession on sunlit soil through the season. Thin seedlings into narrow rows to take advantage of see-through stems. As flowers fade, pull stems out to make way for new. **INVASIVE** in Georgia and Oregon. Alternative: dotted mint (*Monarda punctata*).

Viola labradorica

LABRADOR VIOLET

Viola labradorica

Perennial | Zones 2 to 8

DESCRIPTION Labrador violets are more elegantly refined than their class-clown pansy cousins. They spread via rhizomes and seeds through fully sunny to shady nooks and crannies with small, spurred purple spring flowers dangled over 3- to 6-in. evergreen bouquets of heart-shaped leaves. Leaf color ranges from nearly black-purple to weathered-bronze depending on light and soil conditions. Sister violet (*V. sororia,* zones 3 to 9), also native to eastern North America, has 6- to 8-in. green leaves, robust enough to pair with hosta and heuchera, and spring flowers in purple or white with a gray-blue throat; the flowers of *V. sororia* 'Freckles' are white with purple flecks. Both species' leaves feed fritillary butterfly caterpillars.

FINE PRINT Prefers full sun to shade, and moist soil. Seeds scatter, ejected from pods. Because insect pollination is unreliable, the showy flowers are replaced in summer with hidden cleistogamous or closed, self-pollinating flowers.

Zinnia angustifolia

CREEPING ZINNIA, MEXICAN ZINNIA

Annual

DESCRIPTION Despite how easy zinnias are to start from seed, I never expect them to volunteer and that's why it's such a thrill to see creeping zinnia (not to be confused with the other creeping zinnia, *Sanvitalia procumbens*) pop up again. An endless abundance of 1-in. wide white or bright orange daisies dot the 1-ft. tall clump, also studded with narrow mildew-resistant gray-green leaves from emergence to frost.

FINE PRINT Prefers full sun, and average, well-drained soil. Drought tolerant. Seeds drop. Seedlings emerge late, in early summer when the soil is warm. "Self-cleaning" flowers do not need deadheading to look their best.

Zinnia angustifolia with a petunia hybrid and chartreuse licorice vine.

PLANTS THAT SPREAD

WHEN A
LITTLE
GOES A
LONG
WAY

Gardeners expect most perennials and shrubs to follow the reassuring adage, "the first year it sleeps, the second year it creeps, the third year it leaps." But some plants creep from the get-go and others hit the ground running. Either way, plants that widen their stance by sending up suckers from roots, or by spreading outwards in clumps or via rhizomes and stolons, will graciously fill the garden with broad sweeps of color and texture sometimes sooner than their third year. Growing with the vigor of "weeds," spreaders offer lavish abundance at dime-a-dozen prices, give actual weeds a run for their money, and provide us the chance to grow an extra-exuberant garden. They'll also exercise your green thumbs by allowing the convenience of creative control and the luxury of generosity. Because whenever you have too much of a good thing, all you need to do is divide, transplant, and share.

When I fall for a plant, rather than buying the recommended three, five, or seven of the same variety, I usually tuck in what Plant Delights Nursery owner Tony Avent calls "drifts of one" to see how it grows. I

suspect most of us on a budget do that. It's not wrong, but when the garden is young or sparse it can slow the process of creating a naturally cohesive, rich, and riotous design—unless we make the most of that one by propagating the heck out of it. Some plants will spread vigorously or grow quickly enough to make a new garden or area look established and lush within the first season or two. I put those to work as temporary placeholders that keep my garden growing while I debate all of the design options and plant choices available to me. And as soon as they've matured I buy a little more time by transplanting pieces of their overgrowth wherever they'll provide the dramatic echoing drifts and syncopated rhythms I enjoy so much in other gardens.

Plants that grow by leaps and bounds make a lot of gardeners nervous. We all have a list of plants that we warn our friends about that includes regionally invasive species as well as anything that requires more strength to manage or remove than we have in our arms and legs. We reserve the right to disparage those plants as aggressive thugs, bullies, and the devil. But each of us has a different tolerance threshold. One person's devil is another's favorite groundcover. My definition of groundcover is anything that provides a carpet where I want it to, whether it hugs the ground or has a sizeable presence, and doesn't require a backhoe or flamethrower to edit when it rolls out too far.

Allow a sprig of golden creeping Jenny (*Lysimachia nummularia* 'Aurea') or a burnished silver *Sedum spathulifolium* to ramble along a border, over the curb

and into the street. Those spreaders are too tiny and easy to toss out to be considered bullies by most of us. Pick on something your own size instead, like plume poppy (*Macleaya cordata*)—or let that gray-green, feather-topped 10-footer hold up the back of a border, screen the neighbors, and change the garden's scale from shy and retiring to bold and beautiful. As tall as it is by midsummer, it's easy to manage because its roots are close enough to the surface to be cut out by spade or pulled by hand.

Generous swaths of a single species can offer our eyes a place to land that's more interesting than sweeps of lawn, which functions the same way but requires more attention. In an intensively planted garden, use a foliar giant like butterbur (*Petasites japonicus*) for its restful surface area and engrossing contrast. Because it too is shallow rooted and easy to edit (especially considering its gargantuan leaf size) it can even be enjoyed in a small garden like mine.

As you come to appreciate, rather than fear, plants with exuberant growth habits, take another look around gardens that inspire you and (re)discover

---

OPPOSITE The large oak-like leaves and spires of plume poppy (*Macleaya cordata*) towering over brightly variegated *Brunnera macrophylla* 'Hadspen Cream' give this quiet border something to talk about. BELOW Sweet fern (*Comptonia peregrina*) planted in shallow and dry soil at the entrance of Blithewold's parking lot.

some great plants. Plenty will thrive on benign neglect once established in the right location, with whatever soil type and amount of sun and moisture they require and you happen to have. Mexican evening primrose (*Oenothera speciosa*) and plumbago (*Ceratostigma plumbaginoides*) will brilliantly cover and color any sunny patch of soil. Barrenwort (*Epimedium*) and gingers (European and native species of *Asarum*) will colonize dry shade as if they'd never considered those two conditions to be even remotely difficult. Sweet fern (*Comptonia peregrina*) offers fragrant hip-to-shoulder-high texture on dry sunny slopes where no other hedge would cover the ground as graciously.

Allow spreaders to engage in friendly competition with others that can give as good as they get, or at least hold their own. It would take a heavy hand to do in a healthy daylily, baptisia, or amsonia. Shrubs and sturdy plants with impenetrable crowns can stand like boulders in a running river of grape-leaf anemone (*Anemone tomentosa* 'Robustissima').

Combine early-rising sweet woodruff (*Galium odoratum*) and snow poppy (*Eomecon chionantha*) with slow-to-wake hostas for a succession of textures, or highlight spring by planting them with shrubs that bloom in concert, like blueberry and fothergilla. And let the task of monitoring and controlling their growth become an addicting pastime that reminds you that a garden is an engaging work in process as well as a sweet place to sit in the evenings around the guacamole bowl with friends.

Butterbur (*Petasites japonicus*) rambles along under Black Lace elderberry (*Sambucus nigra* 'Eva') in my moist and shady sideyard garden.

GUIDE TO ABUNDANCE: REUSE, REPLANT, REPEAT

We know we've made the right choices for our garden when plants thrive. Seeing them take hold and increase is gratifying in itself, but managing their progress through the garden offers endless opportunities to actually improve their health and vigor, make adjustments to our garden's design, and come closer by the day to our ideas of Eden.

To include spreaders in your garden, start by allotting new plants the room they'll need as they grow to maturity. Try hard to follow the proper spacing advice on plant tags (how many inches between other plants) even if it looks like your latest acquisition will wedge into a tighter space. If you're not given any hints, allow two or three times the diameter of the crown around a spring- or fall-planted herbaceous perennial. With shrubs it's helpful to know their ultimate mature size and to plan accordingly to give them the space they'll eventually need. By underplanting young shrubs with easily transplantable perennials or disposable self-sown annuals, the space they take up can be endlessly tweaked over the years in which they come into their own.

Once in the ground, a plant's individual rate of growth will determine how it needs to be managed. Some, like mint family runners and clumpers, will want your attention at least annually to remain within bounds and healthy. Others that poke new shoots out of the ground for the better part of the growing season, like plume poppy (*Macleaya cordata*), flowering raspberry (*Rubus odoratus*), and butterbur (*Petasites japonicus*), may require weekly or monthly deletions. Still others, hakonechloa and epimedium for example, grow at such a comparatively leisurely pace that years can pass without requiring any interference from us. No matter how quickly plants grow, your garden will ultimately benefit from hard-hearted chucking of unwanted or unhealthy pieces of your favorite spreaders.

The flip side is that spreaders produce a rich resource of extra pieces that can be planted for instant gratification elsewhere in the garden. Use the easily transplantable suckers, layers, and offshoots of plants like silverbush elaeagnus (*Elaeagnus* 'Quicksilver'), sweet-breath-of-spring (*Lonicera fragrantissima*), and thornless blackberry (*Rubus ulmifolius*) to create a series of focal points, scent centers, or snack stations around the garden. Or divide clump- or mat-forming

A traffic-stopping container combination of Tiger Eyes staghorn sumac, leopard plant (*Farfugium japonicum* 'Aureomaculatum'), *Hakonechloa macra* 'All Gold', and *Begonia* (Million Kisses Series) Devotion.

SOLITARY CONFINEMENT

Gardeners often attempt to confine spreaders by burying barriers (such as pieces of metal or wooden edging and open-bottomed pots) inside the garden. Barriers are an effective way to *temporarily* corral sprawling rhizomatous plants, like mint and butterbur, into tight clumps but I think they are more work than it's worth. Confinement not only entails digging extra-deep holes to sink the barrier, but it doesn't take long for most spreaders to flee the center of their pot, pile themselves up into a thick mat of roots at the edges, and go under, over, and through to escape. It also bears remembering that the more difficult a plant is to manage and remove (such as almost any running bamboo) the more difficult its dense growth will be to dig out from the edges of a barrier. As a general rule, it is much better to plant what you can easily control in the first place, and then monitor and edit your plants as needed.

That said, I planted my mint in a corner, contained on one side by the house foundation and on another by a heavily travelled walkway. It can't go far and smells delicious whenever it does get underfoot. Use natural barriers, like driveways and tree roots to hem in the rambunctious and then watch them like a hawk anyway. Confined or not, mint family thugs (such as beebalm, spearmint, and spotted deadnettle) should be divided and replanted every spring or two to keep them healthy and tidily clumped.

A mint runner. This is why gardeners try to confine it.

perennials—such as mountain mint (*Pycnanthemum muticum*) and betony (*Stachys officinalis* 'Hummelo')—to transplant wherever they'll beat a pattern that marches to your inner drummer. Fill in shady gaps or fill out and embellish your container garden with strawberry begonia (*Saxifraga stolonifera*) and golden Japanese forest grass (*Hakonechloa macra* 'Aureola').

Nothing looks more remarkable in a mixed container than a sucker from a Tiger Eyes staghorn sumac (*Rhus typhina* 'Bailtiger'). Underplant it with

plumbago (*Ceratostigma plumbaginoides*), or any begonia or heuchera, for a partially shady show that will look spectacular in the fall as blue plumbago flowers bounce off the foliage of the sumac as it turns bright orange. When the season is over, plant the sucker back in the garden, pass it along to a friend, or compost it and start over with new suckers next year.

Barrenwort (*Epimedium*) and sweet woodruff (*Galium odoratum*) running together in a shady rock garden.

PROPAGATION: EASY PIECES

Most spreaders can be easily propagated for transplanting, potting up, or passing along to friends by using at least one of three methods:

- **Division:** splitting plants into smaller pieces, each with its own root system. This method works with well-established (at least two-year-old) rhizomatous, stoloniferous, and clump- or mat-forming perennials. Division is also a propagation option for perennials and shrubs that produce offshoots or suckers.
- **Layering:** encouraging adventitious roots to form by placing healthy growing cells in contact with soil. Plants with stems that are flexible enough to be bent and pinned to the ground without snapping are ideal candidates for layering.
- **Sticking root cuttings:** taking pieces of plants' roots and reburying them so they will sprout new shoots. Try this with plants capable of self-propagating the same way—by producing colonies of new shoots from their roots and rhizomes even when pieces have been severed from the parent plant.

Division

Division is the most convenient propagation method for filling gaps in new or existing garden beds. Provided with a little water (and shade if you divide during a sunny heat wave), transplants will settle in quickly and take off, only to need dividing themselves soon enough. In fact, most perennials—whether we or our friends want extra pieces or not—require dividing every two or three years to maintain optimal health and vigor. Otherwise, as new growth circles outward from weakened centers, bloom production begins to slow and plants ultimately look wretched. Division is also necessary to keep any growing garden from becoming overcrowded.

The best time to divide most plants is during the early spring (before the forsythia and daffodils have bloomed their hearts out) because any plant at the start of its growth cycle will be just as happy to start growing elsewhere. This time of year is also easier for division because we will have already cut off stalks and seedheads that could poke us in the nose as we work, and new growth won't yet be up enough to get in the way of our feet. And we can usually count on spring's gentle rain and moderate temperatures to help give plants the transitional care they need before summer's heat arrives.

The exceptions to the divide-in-early-spring rule are the plants that bloom before the summer solstice, such as irises, peonies, woodland and moss phlox, and euphorbia. Divide these and other early-spring bloomers in the fall to give them the winter to settle in and perk back up for their show. (Mulch their crown to help prevent frost heaving during winter's freezes and thaws.) And of course, rules are made to be broken. If you offer plants plenty of water (and shade if they wilt) and if you trim any lush top growth that would tax a reduced root system, you can divide and transplant anything any time you feel the need. Plants might limp along after surgery but they'll be right as rain next season.

To help prevent transplant shock, water your garden before getting started (particularly if the soil is dry and dusty) and then wait for a few days to give plants a chance to absorb enough moisture.

Dividing rhizomatous or clump-forming perennials

Unplant by digging around the perimeter with a spade, and lever the clump out gently as you get underneath it. Try to keep the root zone intact and full of soil while loosening the crown of the plant like a tooth. Listen for the satisfying pops and cracks as it comes free. If the plant is really heavy, leave it in its hole. If you can lift it without putting your back out (always use your thigh muscles), place it on a clear patch of ground or on the lawn.

An early-spring cartful of hakonechloa divisions.

TOP Choosing a midline of a hakonechloa, a rhizomatous perennial. MIDDLE Using the leverage of the forks to force halves apart. BOTTOM Two easy pieces. The one on the left is big enough to split again.

Some plants, like lamb's ear (*Stachys byzantina*) and low-growing groundcovers, will easily tease apart with deft fingers, like loosening a knot from a skein of yarn. But the majority will require a little more elbow grease. The first step is to make an eyeball assessment of the diameter and find a midline. Sometimes an obvious gap is present in the center, in which case separating any portion of the remaining donut will be beneficial for the whole plant. If it hasn't abandoned its center it can be harder to discern where to slice.

Take your best guess and insert two sturdy digging forks, back-to-back along any seam (even if it's invisible). Push the forks into the roots—sometimes this requires the force of a jump to make the tines penetrate. Use the leverage of the two forks, forced apart, to separate clumps. If the root mass is extremely

dense, sever it into pieces using a sharpened spade or a handsaw; cut any joined stems with sharp pruners. Transplant the healthiest pieces, water all of them in, and baby them as if you spent a fortune, which, in a sense, you did if you reckon your time and sweat.

ABOVE Staking a claim to a mat of oregano, a perennial mint family member that spreads radially. BELOW A tidy clump remains after removing the unwanted sections.

Dividing mat-forming perennials

Unplanting isn't always necessary when dividing perennials that form a carpet of growth because any portion can be removed without much disruption to the rest of the plant. Eyeball or mark the part you want to keep, then slide a spade into the mat outside of your markers and dig the extras out in pieces. Fill soil in around the remaining chunk and water well. If the best-looking growth is not where you want it, dig out the entire plant and transplant the healthiest-looking sections.

Dividing suckering shrubs

If shrubs have sent up new suckers from roots, dig around to find where they are attached. Then sever their root connection to the parent plant with pruners

or a sharp spade leaving 1 to 2 feet of root attached to the new division. Sometimes the root will extend from the sucker or shoot in a T, on its way to forming another. Pull all of that out if you do not want another plant to form (even separated from the original parent, that root should be capable of sending up new growth). Slice that root again 1 to 2 feet from your new plant. Suckers do not always have fully formed feeder roots of their own, so after transplanting, keep them well watered at least until they settle in and begin to grow.

To increase a sucker's survival rate, sever the connection to the parent plant in summer or early fall, but let the sucker remain where it is while it produces its own feeder roots. Wait until the following spring to transplant the sucker.

Dividing perennial plantlets and offshoots from stoloniferous shrubs

I am helpless to resist plantlets that have formed at the ends of stolons. If plantlets and offshoots have been in contact with soil and are already rooted, you can simply cut them from the parent and transplant, as you would a sucker. Any that have not yet formed roots only need contact with soil and time to set roots before becoming a full-fledged plant of their own. Leave the umbilical stolon attached to continue supplying nutrients while you give the plantlet or offshoot some loose soil to sit in, and keep it watered. After a week or two (or a month or two depending on the species and time of year) give the plantlet a little tug. If you meet resistance, roots have formed and you may cut the cord. Play it safe and transplant only after it has become visibly larger.

Layering

Some plants leapfrog through the garden, layering themselves in by forming adventitious roots wherever branch elbows or fingertips touch the soil. If a plant can manage such a feat, there's no reason why gardeners shouldn't take advantage of that energy and help them on their way. How do you know if a

Oakleaf hydrangea (*Hydrangea quercifolia*) suckers are easily separated from the parent in early spring before they leaf out.

ABOVE Plantlets dangle from a potted strawberry begonia (*Saxifraga stolonifera*). BELOW Roots formed on this sweet-breath-of-spring (*Lonicera fragrantissima*) branch where it had been buried the previous season. RIGHT Wounding the stem to layer a *Fothergilla gardenii*, which otherwise spreads slowly by suckering.

plant can be layered? Try it. Merely bending a branch downward sets a hormonal ball rolling inside that signals the plant to push out fresh vertical growth. If the versatile cells at the leaf nodes are placed in contact with soil, the plant will usually take the hint and grow roots there.

Late summer into fall is the best time to propagate by layering because most plants will spend their energy on root production before they go into winter dormancy. By spring the rooted layers should be ready for transplanting. Start by digging a little hole and burying the branch tip in the soil. If a branch is really supple, bend it in arches and use a rock to pin the low points, each to include a leaf node, under the soil. Either way, a wounded stem is more likely to trigger

root growth so let it crack slightly under the pressure of your pin (or, before burying the stem, nick the bark on the underside at a leaf node, where roots will form). Leave the branch attached so it can continue to draw energy from the rest of the plant until it makes its own roots. By the next spring or fall, after each bend or branch tip has made enough roots and leaves to support itself, you can sever the connection anywhere along the original branch, dig it out, and transplant it.

Sticking root cuttings

When plants are dormant they store energy in their roots, which are often especially fat and full of carbohydrates in the winter. (Who isn't?) By sticking root cuttings, we can take advantage of their urge to run around the block with that energy come spring. The best choices for this method are plants that aren't easy to divide—such as oakleaf hydrangea, flowering raspberry, or any other large, established shrub—and anything from which you want more pieces than you would get via division. Young thick roots from healthy plants (of any age) will be most capable of sprouting. Start root cuttings during dormancy, after the plant's leaves have fallen or died back to the ground.

Sticking root cuttings from shrubs

Expose some of the shrub's roots before the ground freezes, or during a midwinter thaw, and select a few that are at least pencil-thick and fleshy rather than woody. (Don't be greedy: never remove more than a third from a plant's root system.) Because roots are hormonally oriented to produce new shoots from whichever severed end had been closest to the plant, maintain the roots' polarity by making your first cuts

straight across at right angles to the root so you'll always know which end is up. Chop the root into smaller pieces (3 to 6 inches long) for easy planting and cut the bottom end on an angle to help remind you which end goes down. Make a fresh straight cut at the top of the next section, then an angled cut, and so forth down the root.

Replant the parent, water it in well, and apply a blanket of mulch to keep it from heaving out during winter's cold snaps. Then "stick" the cuttings in a well-drained part of the garden by inserting the root sections vertically into the soil, pointy end down; the cuttings should be 1 or 2 inches below the soil level so that the flat top of the root is covered. If your soil is frozen, you can also root cuttings in containers placed on a cold porch or inside a cold frame. Either

OPPOSITE The wounded branch pinned under a rock to keep it in contact with the soil while roots form. RIGHT A flush cut at the top end of the root and an angled bottom cut helped me keep this root cutting correctly oriented for sticking.

BELOW Sticking Tiger Eyes staghorn sumac root cuttings in potting soil. BOTTOM Perrenial plumbago (*Ceratostigma plumbaginoides*) cuttings prepared for burial under ½ inch of soil. This cluster of roots produced a good-sized clump of sprouts; I transplanted the whole potful to the garden in early summer. BOTTOM RIGHT A plumbago successfully sprouted using the plastic bag method.

way, water the cuttings after sticking and continue to monitor them so they don't dry out or sit in a puddle of water—rot is the most likely reason why root cuttings sometimes fail.

Depending on the species, new shoots may appear months later in spring. Other plants will form a full root system first and only send up shoots when they're good and ready. Give your cuttings plenty of time to grow before moving them—or stick them where you wanted them in the first place. Make sure to label and date your cuttings to keep from planting something else in the same location.

Sticking root cuttings from perennials

Perennials, especially those with shallow root systems, are generally more forgiving about polarity, so it is less important to keep track of which end is up. Select roots that feel fat and healthy and cut them into 2- to 4-inch sections. Space them out horizontally in a container nearly full of dampened potting soil, cover them with another 1/2 inch, and water well. Place

TOOLS FOR PROPAGATING SPREADERS

- **Spades** are flatter than a shovel with rectangular or narrow blades that are easy to insert vertically in crowded beds. They usually have a D-shaped handle at hip height.
- **Digging forks** have four flattened sturdy tines (unlike pitchforks which have three to six thin pointy tines) and are squared off with a D-shaped handle like a spade. Buy two forks or borrow an extra one for dividing.
- **Pruners (secateurs) and loppers** are bypass-bladed tools for severing root connections precisely. They are also used to trim top growth and any stems that might get in the way.
- **Hand saws** are used to prune tree and shrub limbs above ground and to cut through dense mats of roots. Stony soil abuses saw blades so buy two, one for each task.
- **Hori-horis (Japanese digging knives) and trowels** are ideal for levering out small pieces of shallow-rooted plants. The hori-hori's serrated edge is especially useful for sawing through fibrous roots.

A sturdy trowel and hori-hori (shown center, front) along with sharp pruners, loppers, and a saw (like the ones in the trug) are worth the investment to buy new, but look for secondhand spades and digging forks.

them on a chilly porch, in a cold frame, or by the window in a bright room. Cuttings taken over the winter or in early spring and kept cool should start sprouting as temperatures rise in spring. After most or all of them have sprouted shoots, pot them into individual pots to grow stronger before planting them outside.

Another option is to partially fill a plastic grocery bag with dampened potting soil and root cuttings. Hang the bag in a bright place indoors, protected from freezing, check often for new growth and to remoisten the soil if necessary. Transfer cuttings to pots as soon as shoots appear.

A generously spreading hakonechloa and a potted bugle (*Ajuga reptans* 'Burgundy Glow') mingle in this shady border.

50 THRILLING FILLERS

Like all of the choices open to us since plant hunters started traveling the world, spreaders come from far and wide as well as close to home. They range in shape and size from the daintiest ground huggers to giants with leaves the size of umbrellas. They thrive in a wide variety of zones, soil conditions, and light and heat levels. There is something—to dozens of possible somethings—that will look lovely and behave beautifully in every garden.

I have made a note in the plant descriptions whenever a plant's rambunctious growth threatens local environments and has been listed as an invasive threat. If a nearby state is listed, do extra research to find out if you too should avoid the plant. As for behavior, a sliding scale of vigor exists as well. I have also only listed plants that have been easy for me to dig out, divide, or otherwise manage to keep in bounds. To quantify that, I must reveal that I am not much bigger or stronger than a 99-pound weakling, and I'm not getting any younger. But I am reasonably fit and do expect to exert myself from time to time by jumping up and down on digging forks. I have included mention if any of my favorites requires more effort than that.

Look around your garden to identify areas where you can imagine broad swaths of color or texture, and dramatic repeating themes. Imagine using overgrowth as an excuse to cut down on your lawn mowing and make new garden beds. Picture a patio full of gorgeous containers full of plants that cost nothing but a spring or autumn morning of digging and dividing. And then dig in.

Achillea millefolium
YARROW

Achillea millefolium 'Terracotta'

Perennial | Zones 3 to 9

DESCRIPTION Butterflies ride on flat-topped flower clusters that hover above rhizomatous mats of minutely cut, feathery foliage. Countless cultivars are available in warm colors ranging from brilliant yellow 'Moonshine' to rusty red 'Paprika' and sweet 'Pink Grapefruit'. The foliage comes in another range of colors from pewter to grass-green, and stems can be anywhere from 18 to 30 in. tall, growing as wide. Plant yarrow with clary sage and lavender in the herb garden or use it to loosen the tie of a formal border.

FINE PRINT Prefers full sun, and average, well-drained soil. Drought tolerant. Shorten stems by half in spring to encourage them to stand upright. Deadhead to lateral buds for extra blooms or cut entire stems to the ground when flowers fade. Divide in spring or fall.

Alstroemeria
PERUVIAN LILY

Alstroemeria 'Mauve Majesty' with blood flower.

Perennial | Zones 5 to 11 depending on cultivar

DESCRIPTION To grow Peruvian lily means constantly having to make the choice between cutting stems to take indoors (known to last for weeks in water) or enjoying their flamboyant, tiger-striped, azalea-like blooms out in the garden. Breeders have created a wide variety of colors, stem heights (from less than 12 in. to 5 ft.), and even zone hardiness. Ligtu hybrids are grown from seed and will reseed; sterile hybrids form increasing clumps from rhizome-like tubers.

FINE PRINT Prefers full sun to partial shade, and rich, moist soil. Trigger repeat blooms by yanking spent flower stems out from the base—this keeps the clump healthy by opening the crown. Flowering slows when the soil heats up; mulch to keep it cool. Dig deep (about 15 in.) for the tubers and divide them in spring.

Anemone tomentosa 'Robustissima'
GRAPE-LEAF ANEMONE, JAPANESE ANEMONE

Anemone tomentosa 'Robustissima'

Perennial | Zones 5 to 9

DESCRIPTION Robust is right. The 2-ft. wide bushels of soft, palm-sized, deep green leaves pop up from rhizomatous roots here, there, and everywhere in the spring and by mid to late summer wave bobbles of open-faced pinkish purple flower clusters on 3- to 4-ft. tall stems. Let them float around giant-leaved *Hosta* 'Sum and Substance', meander through a shrub border with ninebark (*Physocarpus opulifolius*) and hydrangea, or fill in along a picket fence.

FINE PRINT Prefers sun to partial shade, and average soil. Support the top-heavy stems with neighboring plants or stakes. Edit or propagate by loosening soil with a digging fork and lifting and transplanting clumps in spring or fall.

Arundo donax 'Variegata'
STRIPED GIANT REED

Arundo donax 'Variegata'

Perennial grass | Zones 6 to 9

DESCRIPTION Growing 6 to 12 ft. tall (or more) in a single season, the variegated corn-like stalks are a fantastic focal point among other giants. Pair this white to cream on deep green sky scraper with amaranth, canna, and dinnerplate dahlias to evoke the tropics or use it as a backdrop to soften the edges of buildings and rooflines. If frost comes late to your garden, striped giant reed will be topped with pink flower plumes in mid to late fall.

FINE PRINT Prefers full sun, moist soil, and protection from wind. The variegated form is naturally less vigorous than the straight species and dry soil will slow its growth further. The rhizomes become woody and difficult to dig out over time but it is surprisingly shallow-rooted and can be confined in a container. Cut stems to the ground in late winter. Divide in spring. The straight species is **INVASIVE** in Arizona, California, Georgia, Maryland, Nevada, New Mexico, Texas, and Virginia.

Boltonia asteroides 'Nally's Lime Dots'
FALSE ASTER

Boltonia asteroides 'Nally's Lime Dots' and great burnet.

Perennial | Zones 4 to 9

DESCRIPTION Slender stems of narrow rubbery blue-green leaves lengthen through the summer only to be topped, as the days shorten, by a 6-ft. tall well-branched display of small (1/2 in. diameter) lime-green polka dots that are, in fact, petal-less daisies. I adore this cultivar of a North American native for the generous clumps of airy weirdness it weaves through the garden—and flower arrangements—with petaliferous zinnias and dahlias.

FINE PRINT Prefers full sun, and average, well-drained soil. Stems are top heavy and will bow down after downpours. For a shorter, sturdier show, cut stems in half at least twice before midsummer. Divide clumps in spring.

Carex
SEDGE

Carex morrowii 'Ice Dance' in an evergreen combination at Bedrock Gardens.

Perennial | Zones vary

DESCRIPTION Some gardeners trade in their lawn for lush tufts of sedge. Variegated Japanese sedge (*C. morrowii* 'Ice Dance', zones 5 to 9), being fairly bulky at around 1 1/2 ft. tall, is perhaps better suited to shady borders where it can mingle with hosta and heuchera. But oak sedge (*C. pensylvanica*, zones 4 to 8), also perfectly at home under deciduous trees, makes a sublime 6- to 12-in., color-shifting (from pale green to beige in fall) native substitute for a low-traffic lawn in dry gardens.

FINE PRINT Both species prefer partial shade and average to moist soil and spread politely by rhizomes. In late winter or early spring, remove tattered leaves from clumps of variegated Japanese sedge, and cut oak sedge to the ground. Divide in spring, using a saw if necessary to get through any dense mats of roots.

Ceratostigma plumbaginoides
PLUMBAGO, LEADWORT

Ceratostigma plumbaginoides wanders along a gravel path underneath *Kalimeris incisa* 'Blue Star.'

Perennial | Zones 5 to 9

DESCRIPTION Weed-busting tangles of green-olive foliage emerge late enough in spring to give bulbs a chance to shine and then open gentian-blue flowers from pimento-red buds in late summer. Let it take hold of border fronts with St. John's wort (*Hypericum*) and woolly thyme (*Thymus pseudolanuginosus*) and ramble widely along sunny slopes with bayberry (*Myrica pensylvanica*) and sweet fern. Plumbago foliage turns berry-red in the fall.

FINE PRINT Prefers full sun to partial shade, and average soil. Cut the wiry stems to the ground in late winter. New shoots appear in late spring to early summer. To divide, dig clumps and pull rhizomes apart with your hands. Or propagate via root cuttings.

Chamaemelum nobile
ROMAN CHAMOMILE

Chamaemelum nobile and pink sweet William catchfly.

Perennial | Zones 6 to 9

DESCRIPTION Thick carpets of finely cut green-apple foliage and 12-in. tall daisy-like flowers spread vigorously enough by layering to make a lush lawn substitute or fill in herb garden edges. It is possible to grow the foliage without flowers—certain cultivars are bred to be more lawn-like—but I would miss the he-loves-me–he-loves-me-not blooms that appear at the same time as betony and yarrow.

FINE PRINT Prefers full sun, and average well-drained or sandy soil. Dry the leaves for potpourri and the fully open flowers for a sleep-aid tea and hair lightener. Trim stems by half or mow them in early summer to help keep them from reclining. Divide in spring.

Chrysanthemum 'Sheffield Pink'
HARDY MUM

Chrysanthemum 'Sheffield Pink'

Perennial | Zones 3 to 7

DESCRIPTION Fall without mums would be like Halloween without candy corn: not nearly as sweet. This cultivar's old-fashioned earthy apricot-pink daisy petals sit atop deep green stems that grow 2 to 3 ft. tall, providing the perfect foil for the season's reds, yellows, and blazing orange. Their yellow pollen-heavy centers give the bees and butterflies one of their last decent meals before hibernation.

FINE PRINT Prefers full sun and average soil. Plants are politely clump forming. To protect the crown from freeze damage wait until spring to cut stems to the ground. Then pinch stems by half a couple of times before summer solstice to prevent slouching. Divide in spring. Keep your eyes out for sporty new color mutations.

Clematis heracleifolia

TUBE CLEMATIS, BUSH CLEMATIS

Clematis heracleifolia

Perennial | Zones 4 to 9

DESCRIPTION Politely spreading rhizomatous clumps of fist-sized deep green leaves on leaning 2- to 3-ft. tall stems aren't anything special. But in late summer they're interrupted every 6 to 12 in. by clusters of small, lightly fragrant, deep sea–blue, peeled-open, four-petaled flowers that are followed by curled fiber-optic seedheads. To give this subtle stunner a showy contrast, pair it with hakonechloa and hosta.

FINE PRINT Prefers full sun to part shade, and rich, moist soil. Like its vining cousins, tube clematis does best with a cool root zone, but unlike most others, this plant's large leaves help provide its own shade. Cut stems close to the ground in early spring (it blooms on new wood) and transplant offshoots by early summer or wait until fall.

Clerodendrum trichotomum

HARLEQUIN GLORYBOWER

Clerodendrum trichotomum

Shrub | Zones 7 to 9

DESCRIPTION All noses are drawn like magnets to this elegant single-stemmed 5- to 15-ft. tall suckering shrub in late summer when clusters of bright red calyxes sprout five-petaled, intensely perfumed white stars. In the fall all eyes will be on turquoise berries framed by shiny red sepals. Give this specimen space near an open window —for a natural air freshener—and underplant with a spreading groundcover like plumbago or a dwarf shrub such as *Spiraea japonica* 'Golden Elf'.

FINE PRINT Prefers full sun, and average to moist soil. Flowering on new wood, it may be pruned and artfully shaped in spring. In colder zones, it might die back to the ground. Transplant first-year suckers and seedlings (seeds drop) in spring or fall.

Comptonia peregrina
SWEET FERN

Comptonia peregrina

Shrub | Zones 2 to 8

DESCRIPTION Sweet fern's delicately scented, pale green, rickrack leaves densely pack slender rust-colored stems (2 to 4 ft. tall) that spread by suckers to take hold of inhospitable sites and fix their own nitrogen. Grow it with fellow tough-as-nails North American natives like switchgrass (*Panicum virgatum* 'Heavy Metal') and bearberry (*Arctostaphylos uva-ursi*), and once established, expect it to look healthy even during the hottest, droughtiest summers. Rub crushed leaves on skin and clothing to repel mosquitos.

FINE PRINT Prefers full sun to partial shade, and poor, well-drained, acidic soil. Until established, give it some space without a lot of competition. In early spring, before growth starts, propagate by transplanting small suckers or by taking root cuttings (place 2- to 4-in. sections horizontally 1/2 in. deep in rooting medium).

Conoclinium coelestinum
BLUE MISTFLOWER, HARDY AGERATUM

Conoclinium coelestinum and *Dahlia* 'Crazy Legs'.

Perennial | Zones 5 to 11

DESCRIPTION Reddish knee-to-hip-high stems of green quilted leaves are topped from late summer to frost with dusty-blue petal-less flowers that resemble the tall annual *Ageratum* 'Blue Horizon'. This wildflower from central and southeastern United States willingly fills drainage ditches, pond banks, and rain gardens but it also looks great floating around dahlias and asters in a mixed border with hitchhiking butterflies riding its blue clouds.

FINE PRINT Prefers full sun to partial shade, and average soil. In moist soil, the shallow-rooted rhizomatous clumps will grow like mint and need editing or dividing (in the spring) every couple of years; thirst slows it down.

Cornus sericea
RED-TWIG DOGWOOD

Cornus sericea

Stoloniferous shrub | Zones 3 to 8

DESCRIPTION The best reason to grow North American native red-twig dogwood and its Asian and European cousins is for their winter thickets of colorful stems. The straight species grows 7 to 9 ft. tall with deep red stems and incidental oval leaves that shift from green to red and orange in the fall. Spring flowers are followed by decorative white fruit that birds eat up. 'Flaviramea' has 5- to 6-ft. tall chartreuse stems and a very vigorous habit; red-stemmed 'Baileyi' (6 to 10 ft. tall) isn't stoloniferous and won't spread at all.

FINE PRINT Prefers full sun to partial shade, and average to rich, moist soil. For brightly colored stems, prune a quarter to a third of them to the ground in early spring. To propagate, stick cut stems in potting soil in early spring or sever the connection between parent clump and rooted offshoots in fall and transplant them then or wait until spring.

Cypripedium parviflorum var. *pubescens*
YELLOW LADY'S SLIPPER

Cypripedium parviflorum var. *pubescens*

Perennial | Zones 2 to 9

DESCRIPTION Anyone with these orchids growing freely in their woodland garden will feel like a lottery winner. The early-summer blooms dancing on wide, leafy, 12-in. tall green stems are reminiscent of banana-colored toe-shoes with russet laces. Yellow lady's slippers warrant a spacious and prominent position in the garden, but after flowering they'll require nearby company of native ferns and later-blooming woodland wildflowers like wild bleeding heart to distract your attention from overripe foliage.

FINE PRINT Prefers partial shade, and rich, moist soil. Spreads by rhizomes. Divide in fall and mulch annually (also in fall) with shredded or composted leaves. Yellow lady's slippers are protected by the USDA Natural Resources Conservation Service and it is illegal in some states to collect them from the wild. They are expensive to buy from responsible growers or plant societies so make friends with generous gardeners.

Darmera peltata
UMBRELLA PLANT

Darmera peltata, pondside at Bedrock Gardens.

Perennial | Zones 5 to 7

DESCRIPTION After 2-ft. tall bobbles of early-spring pink flowers fade, notched leaves big enough around (2 ft. or more in diameter) to shelter small children from the rain, rise on 3- to 5-ft. tall petioles. The plant will transport your garden to the tropics or to its native ancient Siskiyou forest where Bigfoot also lives. The leaves, which are inverted at the center like windblown umbrellas, catch water before they shed it and turn bright red and yellow in the fall. Place an umbrella plant offshoot along the bank of a cold stream or pond where it will spread slowly only as far as the soil is moist, or give it its own bog in a tub.

FINE PRINT Prefers partial to full shade; moist, rich soil; and cool summer temperatures to keep its leaves from scorching. Divide and transplant the thick rhizomes in spring.

Elaeagnus 'Quicksilver'
SILVERBUSH ELAEAGNUS

Elaeagnus 'Quicksilver' and *Clematis* 'Roguchi'

Shrub | Zones 2 to 8

DESCRIPTION Come spring, pendant branches of burnished silver foliage are discreetly embellished with yellow four-pointed stars that release a sweetly indiscreet perfume. Plant it in a monochromatic necklace with lamb's ear and rose campion, or with deeply contrasting evergreens and plants with dark foliage like ninebark (*Physocarpus opulifolius*) and *Aster* 'Lady in Black'.

FINE PRINT Prefers full sun, and rich, well-drained soil. Drought and salt tolerant. Unpruned silverbush elaeagnus will grow at least 12 ft. tall and wide, but it may be shaped annually after flowering (flowering occurs on second-year wood). *E.* 'Quicksilver' is a sterile hybrid of *E. angustifolia*. Transplant suckers in spring or fall.

Eomecon chionantha
SNOW POPPY

Eomecon chionantha

Perennial | Zones 7 to 9

DESCRIPTION From spring to early summer, bright white wrinkled poppies hover on 1-ft. tall stems over heart-shaped leaves that have a wavy edge and an amphibious texture. Try planting them along a pond bank (with umbrella plant perhaps) or in a rain garden where the soil stays moist but not overly boggy. They'll spread rapidly in these settings and weave themselves around blueberries and summersweet (*Clethra alnifolia*), and through clumps of turtlehead (*Chelone glabra*) and mats of creeping Jenny.

FINE PRINT Prefers full sun to partial shade, and rich, moist soil. Shallow rhizomes are easy to edit but any buried broken bits will resprout. Snow poppies will go dormant during dry summers. Divide in spring or fall.

Epimedium
BARRENWORT, FAIRY WINGS

Epimedium 'Amber Queen'

Perennial | Zones 4 to 9 depending on species and cultivar

DESCRIPTION Given the exquisiteness of the fairy-like flowers that shiver on wiry stems in early spring—along with the asymmetrically heart-shaped, eyelash-edged leaves—it is easy to understand why some gardeners collect epimediums like orchids. On the other hand, these plants spread willingly enough (even in dry shade) that every enthusiast should be able to part with a rhizome or two. Heights vary from a couple of inches to around a foot, and leaf colors range from chartreuse to green, to mottled, edged, and spotted red, to purple. Plant them in magic carpet–like drifts in a woodland garden with European and Canadian ginger, cranesbill geranium, and sedge.

FINE PRINT Prefers partial or bright shade, and rich, moist to dry, well-drained soil. Cut foliage to the ground in early spring before the flowers uncurl from the crown. Divide in fall, using pruners, a saw, or brute force to break tangled clumps apart if necessary.

Fragaria vesca
WOODLAND OR WILD STRAWBERRY

Fragaria vesca shares a pathway with thyme.

Perennial | Zones 5 to 9

DESCRIPTION Check under deep green triads of deckled-edged leaves for snacks in early summer. The fruit is small and a little mealy but gardeners will always be rewarded with a mouthwatering bite of nostalgia. (Didn't we all pick wild strawberries as kids?) Plant the 4- to 8-in. tufts at the front edges of garden beds and paths and watch them leapfrog along, producing plantlets at the ends of stolons.

FINE PRINT Prefers full sun to partial shade, and rich, moist, well-drained soil. Position stolons to root wherever you want, and transplant plantlets in spring or fall. Plants may self-sow if uneaten fruit drops. Production wanes with age so replace clumps with fresh plantlets every two to three years.

Galium odoratum
SWEET WOODRUFF

Galium odoratum

Perennial | Zones 5 to 8

DESCRIPTION Sweet woodruff should almost be required planting in spring gardens and shady borders. The 6- to 12-in. high deep green leaf whorls add interest running around the bare legs of shrubs and its tiny blown-out-white flowers delicately scent late spring's breezes. Let it form a ground-covering mulch under your blueberries—they'll go well together all summer in the moist shade they both love—or allow it to fill spring's naked spots in your sunniest border. In full summer sun, sweet woodruff will go dormant by the time your later-blooming perennials are ready to take over the show.

FINE PRINT Prefers spring sun and summer shade, and average to moist soil. Divide and transplant in spring or fall.

Geranium macrorrhizum 'Bevan's Variety' mingles with lady fern *(Athyrium filix-femina)*.

Geranium macrorrhizum

CRANESBILL GERANIUM

Perennial | Zones 4 to 8

DESCRIPTION Weeds don't stand a chance under the dense 1-ft. tall canopy of apple-scented, apple-green, palmate leaves. Pink, white, or purplish flowers (depending on cultivar) rise slightly above the leaves in loose clusters for a couple of long spring into summer months. Encourage large swaths to fill in neglected areas or plop the pillowy clumps atop quilts of bugle and Meehan's mint in a shady rock garden.

FINE PRINT Prefers sun to partial shade, and dry to moist, well-drained soil. Drought tolerant. Leaves turn purple-red in the fall but may yellow prematurely during hot, dry summers. Pull crispy leaves out like gray hairs to neaten its appearance. Divide in spring or fall.

Hakonechloa macra

JAPANESE FOREST GRASS

Hakonechloa macra 'Aureola' and catmint.

Perennial grass | Zones 5 to 9

DESCRIPTION For anyone as hooked as I am to this grass, its cascades of shin-high chartreuse can't spread fast enough. No partial-shade-loving companions will look wrong with golden Japanese forest grass (*H. macra* 'Aureola'), but hellebores, *Geranium* 'Rozanne', and *Heuchera* 'Caramel' are especially right. If only it would spread like mint we could plant extra pieces in containers with *Fuchsia* 'Gartenmeister Bonstedt'.

FINE PRINT Prefers partial shade, and rich, moist, well-drained soil. Spreads by rhizomes. Let winter twist and curl its blades before you detach them from the crown with snips or a gentle tug in early spring. Divide and transplant in spring.

Hydrangea quercifolia 'Snowflake'

Hydrangea quercifolia
OAKLEAF HYDRANGEA

Shrub | Zones 5 to 9

DESCRIPTION The coarse-textured, oak-notched leaves set this hydrangea apart from the rest, particularly in fall when they turn the deepest burgundy and purple colors. From late summer to its darkest fall moment, it is also distinguished by top-heavy conehead panicles of flowers ('Snowflake' is an exquisite double form) that shift from pale green to white to pink to brown. Winter is this southeastern United States native's only downside: the peeling bark, which is supposed to be "interesting," combined with brown flowers turn it into a tattered ragamuffin. So let it spread its underground stolons in a partially shady border with a distracting clump or two of red-twig dogwood.

FINE PRINT Prefers full sun to partial shade, and rich, moist, well-drained soil. Flowers form on old wood so prune it right after flowering. Sever offshoots from the parent clump and transplant them in spring or fall. Or propagate by taking cuttings or layering in midsummer.

Itea virginica
VIRGINIA SWEETSPIRE

Itea virginica 'Henry's Garnet' and anise hyssop seedheads.

Shrub | Zones 5 to 9

DESCRIPTION I always forget to notice this northeast native shrub's drooping sausage-like racemes of white flowers that bloom through the busy days of early summer, but I never miss the fall show when its translucent leaves blaze red, hanging like pennants on suckering stems. Plant the 2- to 3-ft. dwarf Little Henry (*I. virginica* 'Sprich'), or its 3- to 4-ft. tall cousin, 'Henry's Garnet', in front of feathery autumn flowering grasses and cerulean-blue bog sage—and wherever else its foliage will be back-lit by autumn's low-slung sun.

FINE PRINT Prefers full sun to partial shade, and moist to wet soil. Propagate by cuttings anytime or by division of suckers in spring or fall. Rejuvenate by cutting older stems to the ground in early spring.

Lamium maculatum
SPOTTED DEADNETTLE

Lamium maculatum 'Shell Pink'

Perennial | Zones 4 to 8

DESCRIPTION Spreading by both rhizomes and stolons, this mint family member reaches its silver-centered foliage and knobby spikes of whorled flowers in all directions from spring through summer. A wide assortment of cultivars sport leaves with different patterns from all-green to chartreuse to streaked silver to almost entirely silver, and flower colors ranging from white or yellow to pale pinks and purples. The more green the leaves, the more vigorous the plant; plant spotted deadnettle around shrubs, hosta, and golden Japanese forest grass that can't be run over.

FINE PRINT Prefers partial shade to shade, and moist soil. Spotted deadnettle is very shallow rooted and easy to pull or spade out. Divide in early spring or fall and reposition sections if it piles itself up against roadblocks or goes bald in patches.

Liriope muscari
LILY TURF

Liriope muscari with hosta and heuchera in Blithewold's Moongate Bed.

Perennial | Zones 6 to 10

DESCRIPTION Tufted straps of narrow, deeply ever-green, 1-ft. tall foliage spread from stolons to form a thick pelt even in dry shade under deciduous trees. Late-summer spikes of bluish purple flowers are followed in fall through winter by glossy black berries arrayed on the same narrow tines. Give them room to exhibit their no-frills frills, and contrast with heuchera, epimedium, and plumbago.

FINE PRINT Prefers partial shade, and average rich, acidic soil. Drought tolerant. Cut foliage to the ground in early spring, with a mower or snips, before new growth emerges from the center of each tuft. Divide clumps in early spring or fall.

Lonicera fragrantissima

SWEET-BREATH-OF-SPRING, WINTER HONEYSUCKLE

Syrphid fly visiting flowers of *Lonicera fragrantissima* in early spring.

Shrub | Zones 4 to 8

DESCRIPTION A non-climbing tangled thicket of branches with small, round, almost evergreen leaves extend in 10-ft. arcs to the ground. From late winter into spring, even when the air is cold and noses are frozen, pairs of tiny, disheveled, cream-colored flowers appear at the leaf axils to fill each breath with the sweetest citrusy perfume. Bees love it and birds go for the tiny berries that follow. Plant it in a hedgerow or border with showier shrubs like flowering raspberry and ninebark (*Physocarpus opulifolius*) or banked by perennials and annuals.

FINE PRINT Prefers full sun to partial shade, and average soil. Prune back to a low framework or to the ground after flowering to keep the shrub from looking gangly. Spreads by rooted layers and suckers, either of which may be transplanted in spring or fall, and by bird-strewn seed in some areas. **INVASIVE** in Tennessee and Virginia.

Lysimachia nummularia 'Aurea'

GOLDEN CREEPING JENNY, MONEYWORT

Lysimachia nummularia 'Aurea'

Perennial | Zones 4 to 8

DESCRIPTION Golden creeping Jenny is a pot of gold at the end of the garden's rainbow. Low piles of coinage, to 2 in. high, scatter along the surface of the soil or cascade richly over edges. Use it to fill in naked gaps between flower beds and the lawn edge (be aware that it is likely to creep onto the lawn, though some of us won't mind) or as a weed barrier under roses and along pond banks.

FINE PRINT Prefers full sun to bright shade—foliage will be blazing yellow in full sun and chartreuse in shade—and rich, moist to boggy soil. Spreads by layering. Watch for signs of reversion to the straight species and destroy any deep green portions. Divide and transplant in spring. The straight species is **INVASIVE** in Connecticut, the District of Columbia, Indiana, Maryland, Michigan, Missouri, New Jersey, Oregon, Pennsylvania, Tennessee, Virginia, West Virginia, and Wisconsin.

Macleaya cordata
PLUME POPPY

Macleaya cordata

Perennial | Zones 4 to 8

DESCRIPTION Towering feather-topped stems of gray-green, oak-lobed leaves grow 8 to 10 ft. tall from shallow rhizomes to screen the neighbors, embellish bare walls, and alter the scale of the garden by making us look up. Plant it in a larger-than-life tropical combination with canna and elephant's ears or with the feathery foliage of bronze fennel as an elegantly contrasting summer backdrop along a wide border.

FINE PRINT Prefers full sun to partial shade; average to moist, well-drained soil; and protection from drought and wind. Shallow rhizomes are easy to pull but are brittle and will resprout if broken. Propagate by transplanting root sections or taking root cuttings in spring.

Mahonia aquifolium
OREGON GRAPE,
HOLLY-LEAVED BARBERRY

Mahonia aquifolium 'Smaragd'

Shrub | Zones 6 to 9

DESCRIPTION The holly-like leaf sets on unbranching stems are handsome enough, especially as they change color in the fall, but what makes this slow-growing, 3- to 8-ft. tall suckering shrub so cool are the fragrant clusters of lemon-yellow flowers that appear on the stem tips in early spring and the subsequent blue-black "grapes." Oregon grape is ubiquitous in its native Pacific Northwest and adaptable to dry soil and sunny sites there; elsewhere it is less common and therefore an eye-catching addition to shrub borders underplanted with wild strawberry, snow poppy, or spotted deadnettle.

FINE PRINT Prefers partial shade, and rich, moist, well-drained soil. Protection from winter sun and wind, and from summer drought, will prevent its leaves from looking blowtorched. To propagate, transplant shallow-rooted suckers in spring. Minimize root disturbance by keeping plenty of soil around the roots. Trim the top growth and keep suckers well-watered until established.

Meehania cordata

MEEHAN'S MINT, CREEPING MINT

Meehania cordata

Perennial | Zones 5 to 8

DESCRIPTION The thick mats of green heart-shaped leaves will probably go unnoticed until out-of-scale, tubular, two-lipped lavender-blue flowers emerge in abundant 4- to 6-in. spires in late spring. Beat that, bugle. In fact, indigenous to eastern United States woodlands, it is a native plant-lover's alternative to bugle (*Ajuga reptans*) and spotted deadnettle. Let it run wild through a woodland wildflower garden or along the edges of a shady border planted with hellebores, corydalis, and primroses.

FINE PRINT Prefers partial to full shade, and rich, moist, well-drained soil. Meehan's mint spreads by stolons that trail along the ground and root in as they go. Transplant rooted sections in early spring or fall.

Mentha spicata 'Kentucky Colonel'

SPEARMINT

Mentha spicata 'Kentucky Colonel' with a few 'Alaska Salmon' nasturtiums.

Perennial | Zones 5 to 9

DESCRIPTION This quintessential julep mint sends up lush spears of extra-aromatic quilted leaves from generously spreading shallow-rooted rhizomes until off-white spikes of midsummer flowers cause it to slacken its pace. Plant it with tomatoes and cabbage (it is said to improve their flavor and repel pest insects) or allot it a corner of the herb garden to run circles around clumps of echinacea and lavender.

FINE PRINT Prefers full sun to partial shade, and moist soil. If you choose to contain mint's runners in a pot, buried or above ground, do not let the potting soil dry out. Divide and replant annually to keep it from circling the edges. If you throw caution to the wind and let mint run free (as I do), simply pull or spade out unwanted pieces. Divide in spring or fall.

Monarda didyma
BEEBALM, BERGAMOT

Monarda didyma 'Jacob Cline'

Perennial | Zones 4 to 9

DESCRIPTION You won't need to keep the hummingbird feeder filled while this eastern North American stream bank and wet woodland wildflower is in bloom. Carousels of bright red or pink tubular feeding ports are offered atop ever-increasing clumps of minty fragrant 3- to 5-ft. stems in midsummer. The especially tall cultivar 'Jacob Cline' has fire engine–red flowers and resistance to the powdery mildew fungus that plagues the species. Plant for distraction and entertainment by the kitchen window, or next to your favorite garden bench with other hummingbird magnets like blue anise sage and flowering tobacco.

FINE PRINT Prefers full sun to partial shade, and moist, well-drained soil. Spreads by rhizomes. Deadhead to prolong the bloom time or leave seedheads standing for the birds to eat through the winter. Cut stems to the ground in spring. Divide in spring.

Oenothera speciosa
MEXICAN EVENING PRIMROSE

Oenothera speciosa 'Siskiyou'

Perennial | Zones 5 to 8

DESCRIPTION There is no middle ground with southwest native Mexican evening primrose. Gardeners either love that the fragrant pink-veined cups will open in the daylight for weeks of early summer—even in poor soil during a drought—or hate that it travels at the speed of light and pops up in the middle of neighboring plants. Use it to its and your best advantage by planting it where other plants would fail to thrive: ask it to edge out the weeds along the driveway or pathways where its rhizomatous spread is checked by pavement, or allow it to tumble along under peonies or roses, which aren't the least bit bothered by encroaching runners. The cultivar 'Siskiyou' is very floriferous and grows about 10 in. tall.

FINE PRINT Prefers full sun and any well-drained soil (poor sandy soil slows its growth while rich soil encourages it to run faster). Overly wet winters and poor drainage will do it in. Cut stems back after flowering. Divide in spring.

Orostachys iwarenge
CHINESE DUNCECAP

Orostachys iwarenge in a hypertufa trough with a variety of sedums.

Succulent perennial | Zones 5 to 10

DESCRIPTION Tiny pinkish gray rosettes masquerade as pockets of gravel until 4- to 6-in. creamy-pink flower towers rise like miniature skyscrapers. Tuck them into rock wall crevices where they will also drop themselves in pieces along its base, and among the stones, sedums, and alpines in a sunny rock garden scree.

FINE PRINT Prefers full sun, and poor, well-drained soil. The rosettes are monocarpic—they die after flowering—but produce so many offshoots, you'd never know to miss them. Propagate by digging clusters, gently pulling them apart, and replanting the pieces.

Petasites japonicus and Black Lace elderberry.

Petasites japonicus
BUTTERBUR

Perennial | Zones 5 to 9

DESCRIPTION The green flower clusters that appear in early spring like butter pats on a bed of lettuce give no hint of what follows. Within a couple of weeks after flowering, enormous round leaves, mostly over 2 ft. wide, grow on 3- to 4-ft. tall celery-like stalks from shallow rhizomes. Planting butterbur in a distant corner will pull the area visually closer. Or enjoy their tropical vibe nearby, paired with the lush foliage of viburnum, hydrangea, and red-twig dogwood. 'Variegata' brightens shady borders with smaller white-splashed leaves and a slightly shorter stride.

FINE PRINT Prefers partial to full shade, and moist soil. Leaves may wilt and look wretched during dry spells. Rhizomes are shallow and soft enough to pull out by hand or slice through with a spade. Divide in spring (when the leaves begin to emerge) or fall.

Phlox paniculata
SUMMER PHLOX, GARDEN PHLOX

Phlox paniculata 'Natural Feelings'

Perennial | Zones 4 to 8

DESCRIPTION Fragrant cumulonimbus flower clusters in a range of colors—from sunrise and sunset pinks to storm-cloud lavender and bright white—are tethered to stiff 3- to 5-ft. stems of lance-shaped leaves. The presence of this eastern United States native is practically required in any sunny border so it's lucky for us plant geeks that odd cultivars with showy bracts exist. Look for the pink-and-green 'Natural Feelings' and 'Mystique Black' which has deep purple buds that slowly open to a more normal purplish pink. Surround summer phlox with plants like aster and anise hyssop that can help hide their sometimes mildewy stems.

FINE PRINT Prefers full sun to partial shade, and rich, moist soil. New cultivars are bred for mildew resistance but it is still a good idea to cut about a third of the stems to the ground in early summer to increase airflow through the clump. At the same time, cut some stems in half to stagger their bloom time. Divide in spring or fall.

Phlox stolonifera
CREEPING PHLOX

Phlox stolonifera

Perennial | Zones 4 to 8

DESCRIPTION In early spring, masses of 1-in. wide fragrant pale purple or pink flowers hover on delicate 6-in. stems over dense green mats that elegantly fill swaths of woodland garden floor. Plant creeping phlox or lavender-blue woodland phlox (*P. divaricata*), which is another 6 in. taller but doesn't spread as vigorously, with wild bleeding heart, woodland ferns, daffodils, and trout lily (*Erythronium americanum*). Like the best spring ephemerals, the plants all but disappear from our sight after the flowers go, but their green mats will continue to outcompete weeds. Both creeping and woodland phlox are native to the United States.

FINE PRINT Prefers morning sun and afternoon shade, and rich, moist, well-drained soil. Cut spent flowers back to encourage fresh foliage growth or leave them until early the following spring. Divide any time after flowering.

Porteranthus trifoliatus, syn. *Gillenia trifoliata*
BOWMAN'S ROOT, INDIAN PHYSIC

Porteranthus trifoliatus

Perennial | Zones 5 to 9

DESCRIPTION A delicate rhizomatous native North American filler for beds that are shaded from midday sun. It reaches 2 to 3 ft. tall and about as wide over time with serrated bronze-tinged leaves held on skinny burgundy stems. In late spring, loose five-pointed white stars flutter out of pinkish red calyces looking for all the world like a swarm of butterflies. Although it goes quiet over the summer, the leaves turn shades of peach to red in fall. Plant with other spring bloomers like cranesbill geranium, which has foliage that turns purplish in the fall, and blue star (*Amsonia hubrichtii*) famous for its yellow autumn blaze.

FINE PRINT Prefers partial shade, and rich, moist, well-drained soil. Drought tolerant once established. Propagation by division is tricky because the roots resent disturbance. Try transplanting small pieces in spring or take cuttings instead.

Pycnanthemum muticum
MOUNTAIN MINT

Pycnanthemum muticum

Perennial | Zones 4 to 8

DESCRIPTION This plant, native to eastern North American woodlands and meadows, might not be showy but it is certainly attractive. Dozens of different species of pollinating bees, wasps, butterflies, and moths will congregate to feed on the nectar-rich white flowers arrayed around gray-green buttons set 3 to 5 ft. atop bracts of silver. At home in woodland dapple, mountain mint will also be perfectly comfortable in unfussy sunny borders with goldenrod, beebalm, and betony. Sturdy seedheads remain attractive all winter—to us and to any birds needing cover—and the delicious-smelling minty stems contain a chemical that repels mosquitos when rubbed on bare skin.

FINE PRINT Prefers full sun to partial shade, and rich, well-drained soil. Mountain mint contains the mint family gene for vigor but increases its girth annually in mat-forming increments rather than by runners. Divide in spring or remove a few inches of growth from the perimeter to make room for more.

Rhus typhina 'Bailtiger'
TIGER EYES STAGHORN SUMAC

Rhus typhina 'Bailtiger' spreading through a mixed border.

Shrub | Zones 4 to 8

DESCRIPTION Sculptural antler-furred winter stems disappear under finely cut tiers of key-lime foliage that turn safety-orange in the fall. Growing 6 to 12 ft. tall, Tiger Eyes staghorn sumac can be used as an eye-catching focal point in a wide mixed flower border or as an ornament along the garden's fringes. Suckers spend most of their first season low to the ground as excellent companions for heuchera and catmint (*Nepeta racemosa*), and grow their legs the following season. The straight species of staghorn sumac is often maligned as a weed but I cheer on this eastern North American native whenever it goes head to head with exotic invasive species.

FINE PRINT Prefers full sun to partial shade, and dry to moist, well-drained soil. When grown in partial shade, leaves will be more chartreuse than yellow and fall color will be more reliably orange. Transplant suckers in spring and keep them well-watered through a wilty transition. Or propagate via root cuttings.

Rosa rugosa

BEACH ROSE, JAPANESE ROSE

The brightly colored *Rosa rugosa* among Shasta daisies.

Shrub | Zones 2 to 9

DESCRIPTION Roses have a reputation for being high-maintenance headaches but anything that grows willingly in beach sand must be made of tough stuff. Blackspot avoids this rose's leathery wrinkled leaves and evidently even the buds intimidate aphids and Japanese beetles—perhaps the same way the super thorny stems prevent the gardener from getting too close and fussing. Whether you grow it for the spicy scent of its single cerise or white flowers or for its huge red vitamin C–rich hips, it will look gorgeous alongside calamint, lavender, and Shasta daisies.

FINE PRINT Prefers full sun and any soil. Cut stems back to a low (12- to 18-in.) framework in early spring, before or soon after the foliage buds break. Also in early spring, propagate by transplanting suckers, using a spade (and persistence) to dig out the deep roots.

A double-flowering form of *Rubus odoratus*.

Rubus
BRAMBLE

Shrub | Zones vary

DESCRIPTION After beach roses, I draw the line at thorny briars and brambles. But I do love a good berry pie—lucky for me, not all blackberries require body armor. Thornless blackberry (*Rubus ulmifolius*, zones 6 to 9) will be most productive tied up to a trellis in the vegetable garden but may be allowed to wander through a flower border where second-year canes will offer the weeder sustenance in mid to late summer. Flowering raspberry (*R. odoratus*, zones 3 to 7) and thimbleberry (*R. parviflorus*, zones 3 to 9)), native to eastern and western North America respectively, both provide 3- to 8-ft. tall curtains of velvety grass-green maple foliage that quickly conceal naked ground and screen the view. Flowering raspberry displays clusters of 2-in. wild rose flowers all summer and scant gritty berries best left to the birds; thimbleberry grows sideways at a slightly slower rate while producing white flowers that bloom in early summer and tastier berries. All three plants shed their leaves in winter leaving a lattice-like thicket of stems.

FINE PRINT All prefer full sun (for best flowering and fruiting) to partial shade, and moist soil. For thornless blackberry, cut the past season's productive canes to the ground in late winter or early spring leaving the newest canes for the coming season; trim first-year shoots in spring to encourage branching. For flowering raspberry and thimbleberry, prune top growth and remove shallow-rooted runners as needed. Propagate all by transplanting runners in the fall.

Salvia uliginosa
BOG SAGE

Salvia uliginosa

Perennial | Zones 6 to 10

DESCRIPTION Slender, light green, 4- to 6-ft.stems with smallish leaves branch into airy clumps that wave short spires of sky-blue and white flowers in midsummer to fall breezes. Allow bog sage to spread its shallow rhizomes through the back of a border against a backdrop of canna, to weave through the chartreuse foliage of Tiger Eyes staghorn sumac, or to run pondside with red-twig dogwood.

FINE PRINT Prefers full sun to partial shade, and moist soil (growth will be stunted and its reach limited in dry soil). Divide and transplant in spring, or propagate by tip cuttings in late spring or late summer.

Saxifraga stolonifera

STRAWBERRY BEGONIA, MOTHER OF THOUSANDS

Saxifraga stolonifera

Perennial | Zones 6 to 9

DESCRIPTION Neither a strawberry nor a begonia, its rounded, fuzzy, silver-veined leaves are vaguely begonia-ish, while the plantlets that form at the ends of dangling red stolons are decidedly strawberry-like. Bunches of foliage hug shady ground and send shooting-star flowers skyward on loose 1-ft. tall stems in early summer. Position "mother of thousands" where her daughters can dangle over the edge of a shady rock wall with corydalis and climbing snapdragon, or plant it in containers.

FINE PRINT Prefers partial shade to shade, and rich, moist soil. Propagate by placing plantlets on soil and wait two or three weeks until roots have formed before severing the parental connection. Potted plants can be brought indoors for the winter to dangle in an east window.

Sedum

STONECROP

Sedum dasyphyllum in flower.

Succulent perennial | Zones vary

DESCRIPTION With more than four hundred species to choose from there has to be a stonecrop for every sunny garden. *S. acre* (zones 3 to 8) is famous for covering acres as lushly as lawn although it can't take heavy foot traffic or soccer games. *S. dasyphyllum* (zones 3 to 7) makes tiny mounds of miniscule pinkish gray leaves that break off to make new tiny mounds, and produces clusters of the palest pink flowers on 1- to 3-in. stems in early summer. Dusty gray rosettes and bright yellow star flowers of *S. spathulifolium* (zones 5 to 9) can handle a little shade to look like exquisite beadwork at the garden's fringes.

FINE PRINT Prefers full sun, and average, neutral to alkaline, well-drained soil. Propagate sedums by accidentally or intentionally breaking leaves and letting them fall on the soil where they will eventually root, or divide them in spring.

FALSE SPIREA

Sorbaria sorbifolia 'Sem'

Sorbaria sorbifolia 'Sem'

Multi-stemmed shrub | Zones 2 to 7

DESCRIPTION While the straight species is generally considered too coarse and boring for gardens, 'Sem' is almost too interesting. From spring into early summer the 3- to 4-ft. tall suckering mound of finely cut blushed-peach foliage calls attention to itself like madras plaid shorts on a tourist. The foliage quiets down to ferny green right around the arrival of vanilla-soft-serve flowers in early summer. It is short enough to include in mixed borders underplanted with forget-me-not and blue fescue or to use as an eye-catching filler in a shrub border with ninebark (*Physocarpus opulifolius*) and Black Lace elderberry (*Sambucus nigra* 'Eva').

FINE PRINT Prefers full sun to partial shade, and moist, well-drained soil. Flowering occurs on new wood so stems can be cut to the ground in spring to keep them from getting out of scale. Divide suckers and transplant in spring or fall.

BETONY

Stachys officinalis 'Hummelo'

Stachys officinalis 'Hummelo'

Perennial | Zones 5 to 8

DESCRIPTION Introduced by the master of year-round garden design, Piet Oudolf, and named for his hometown in the Netherlands, 'Hummelo' betony has something for every season. Stoloniferously spreading evergreen clumps of rough but lustrous green foliage look their best in spring and give rise to 2-ft. tall abundant midsummer cob-ettes of intensely purple flowers, which in turn become sturdy seedheads that carry their drifts through fall and winter. The plants are so upright, tidy, and static they look best with anything that moves in the breeze, be it Mexican feather grass or sea holly, butterflies or bumble bees.

FINE PRINT Prefers full sun, and average well-drained soil. Drought tolerant. Like its cousin lamb's ear (*S. byzantina*), 'Hummelo' requires sharp winter drainage but its leathery leaves make it more tolerant of overhead watering. Divide and transplant in spring.

Tetrapanax papyrifer 'Steroidal Giant'
RICE PAPER PLANT

Tetrapanax papyrifer 'Steroidal Giant'

Tree, shrub, or herbaceous perennial (depending on hardiness) | Zones 6 to 11

DESCRIPTION If you really want to impress the neighbors, plant 'Steroidal Giant' where it will make coppiced Paulownia tree leaves look weensy, and cannas—kid stuff. Just don't plant it too near the boundary fence. Enormous raw silk pinwheels (1 to 3 ft. in diameter) produced through the summer on brown felted trunks that rise anywhere from 5 to 12 ft. will certainly cause jaws to drop in awe and envy. But the neighbors might give you the hairy eyeball if its suckers start popping up in their yard.

FINE PRINT Prefers full sun to partial shade, and average, well-drained soil. In zones colder than 8, plants will die to the ground in winter. In warmer zones, height can be restricted by cutting it to the ground in early spring or by replacing older plants with pups. Transplant suckers in spring.

Tiarella
FOAMFLOWER

Tiarella 'Elizabeth Oliver'

Perennial | Zones vary

DESCRIPTION North American native foamflower is too sweet to ever be called aggressive or invasive yet some species and cultivars are vigorous enough to satisfy our craving for more. The East's heart-leaf foamflower (*T. cordifolia*, zones 3 to 8) spreads its blanket of soft green leaves, sometimes marked with maroon streaks, and frothy flowers along the ground via underground stolons. Others, such as *T. wherryi* (zones 3 to 7) from the Appalachian Mountains, and the Pacific Northwest's *T. trifoliata var. laciniata* (zones 4 to 7) form clumps. Hybrid crosses introduced in the 1980s and 1990s like 'Elizabeth Oliver' (zones 4 to 8) have been endlessly tweaked to produce a wide variety of leaf shapes, leaf colors, flower production (though all are either white or pink), and vigor perfect for adding elegance to woodland vignettes of celandine poppy, cranesbill geranium, and lungwort (*Pulmonaria*).

FINE PRINT Prefers partial shade to shade, and rich, moist, well-drained soil. Protect from slugs and excessive winter wetness. Divide and transplant in spring, making sure not to bury the crown.

FROST-
TENDER
PLANTS

❧

PUSH THE
ZONE

I f you are willing and able to make winter accommodations for plants that wouldn't otherwise survive in your climate, you'll open the garden door to a much wider world of possibilities. Tropical plants, frost-tender succulents, and perennials from temperate climates offer fresh and unusual elements otherwise lacking in an exclusively hardy palette of perennials and shrubs. Welcome exotic contrasts, scents evocative of faraway vacations, and a full-spectrum of flowers that promise a color boost just when spring-loaded gardens need it most. And then enjoy how they defy all expectations and extend the initial extravagant display through the heat of summer and well into fall.

Any plant that offers well-timed weeks or months of interest is inherently valuable, but when given winter protection—on sunny living room windowsills, in bright enclosed porches and cold frames, or in dark, cool basements—tender plants become true keepers that are as worthy of their purchase price as any hardy perennial or shrub wintering outside. It is perfectly reasonable to expect them to survive and enrich the garden for years. And just as with self-sowers and

LEFT The color of *Dahlia* 'Uptown Girl' intensifies in the golden light of fall. RIGHT African blue basil (*Ocimum* 'African Blue') catches the long light in Blithewold's Pollinator Garden. PREVIOUS PAGE By tucking canna, pineapple lily, and dahlias amid drifts of kniphofia and grasses, the owners of this temperate-zone garden get to spend late summer in the tropics.

Make a wreath of succulent cuttings, like this one at Avant Gardens, to bring inside for the winter.

spreaders, by taking advantage of their vigor via propagation, you can grow more than you paid for to keep the garden stocked with exotics and share your favorites with friends. There's no (good) reason to ever let the garden—or your interest in it—fade.

I wasn't always so sure about that. When I left the long, mild seasons of the West Coast to return home to the wintery East, I said goodbye to the plants I had relied on as hardy perennials. I assumed my days of gardening with fuchsias, salvias, phormium, Spanish lavender, and rosemary were over. Then I began working with horticulturists at Blithewold who are expert in the art of using tender plants to keep the gardens in peak bloom from spring's start to fall's killing frost, even on a tight nonprofit budget. In late summer and fall, visitors—passionate gardeners and regulars among them—seem genuinely surprised to "still" see so much color and pollinator activity in the gardens that I now help design. Their surprise is a shame though. As glad as I am to accept any portion of the compliments, I am convinced that every gardener could and should take a long, spectacular season for granted.

You can count on blue anise sage (*Salvia guaranitica*) and pink porterweed (*Stachytarpheta mutabilis*) that start out in spring as rooted cuttings in 4-inch pots, to grow 3 feet tall by midsummer. Dahlias that go into the ground in early summer as tubers just breaking dormancy, bloom by late summer and won't quit until the hardest frost. Grow African blue basil (*Ocimum* 'African Blue') for its purple-tinged leaves and blooms that glow in the slanted light of fall, rather than for its culinary qualities. Let it fill in around echinacea seedheads and give the bees a reason to keep working. Take cuttings in the fall for next year's garden and take cuttings from your cuttings in spring to grow even more.

Plant *Fuchsia* 'Gartenmeister Bonstedt' to feed the hummingbirds before they migrate and let a collection of tender ferns and begonias decorate a shady corner of the deck. Grow rosemary (*Rosmarinus officinalis*), lemon verbena (*Aloysia triphylla*), and Spanish lavender (*Lavandula stoechas*) in your herb garden. Keep them in their pots for easy fall relocation to the porch or basement, or give them the season to become lush in the ground—they won't need to be watered as frequently—before potting them back up to bring inside.

Angel's trumpets (*Brugmansia*) make outstanding container plants but they'll be even more outrageous planted in the ground. Find a spot in dappled shade or morning sun with rich soil that stays moist and let it dangle its enormous citrus-scented trumpets over hostas, or plant it to contrast with the tinier trumpets of flowering tobacco (*Nicotiana*). If your garden, or a part of your garden, doesn't ever fall below freezing, you may be able to overwinter your angel's trumpet with a heavy cover of mulch. Otherwise, dig it up or take cuttings to bring inside for the winter.

Plant a necklace of tender succulents—try echeveria, kalanchoe, and aeonium—at the sunny edges of your walkways and patio and then bring them inside to a sunny south window where they might be persuaded to bloom over the winter. Place scented geraniums (*Pelargonium*) in your rose garden as aphid-deterring companions or next to your favorite bench where you can stroke their aromatic leaves to release their scent. Cut them back to bring inside for the winter, root those cuttings, and dry some leaves for sachets.

From midsummer through fall, every garden still has tremendous energy and potential. Give in to the temptation of frost-tender and exotic species, and plan for a succession of color, curious textures, delicious scents, and pollinator entertainment that will sustain you through the lean months and even well into winter.

A potted *Alocasia* 'Calidora' (colocasia's cousin) shines in a shady foundation border.

n order to grow a late-season garden that is larger than life and full of it, you'll simply have to remember to allocate some space in early summer for the small starts that will become full-grown late bloomers well before summer's end. Here are some tricks to finding room for frost-tender keepers even as the garden fills to bursting with plants that self-sow and spread.

Remove early bloomers. Spring and early-summer volunteers like forget-me-not (*Myosotis sylvatica*) and white lace flower (*Orlaya grandiflora*) will no longer need their space after setting seed. Remove early bloomers after they've gone by, making sure to scatter their seeds, and tuck tropicals and tender perennials in the vacancies.

Carve out space between spreaders. Use division of spreading perennials as an excuse to open new slots, graciously sized to accommodate late-season color.

Making room in a spring garden that includes lady's mantle (*Alchemilla mollis*), *Tulipa* 'Cistula', *Hydrangea paniculata* 'Limelight', woodland phlox (*Phlox divaricata*), and a freshly divided Siberian iris.

Use tulips as placeholders for keepers. The timing is right: tulip foliage will wither as the temperatures warm past the danger of frost, exactly when warm-season heat-lovers should be planted. Fork the tulip bulbs out after the foliage has had a chance to die back, to open a patch of earth that is loose and easy to plant in. (Store the dormant bulbs dark and dry for the summer, and replant them in the same loose soil in the fall after rotating the keepers out for storage. Or start over then with new colors.) If you'd rather leave your tulips in the ground, plant over the top and around them, being extra-careful to avoid slicing through the bulbs with your trowel.

Plant keepers in containers. Not only will it be more efficient to move containerized plants in and out at the start and end of the season, but they will look great grouped on the deck with other potted annuals, hardy perennials, and shrubs. Sometimes too, a single pot achieves an even better effect out in the garden. A glory bush (*Tibouchina urvilleana*) in full purple burst or a large-leaved elephant's ear (*Colocasia*) can provide a focal point if one is lacking. You can also use pots of felicia, dahlia, abutilon, and begonia, to name a few, to plug holes as other plants fade out of favor or bloom.

PROPAGATION: BEG A CUTTING

Rather than blowing the budget on a flat of coleus, buy one of everything you like and grow a dozen more of each. Take advantage of spring growth spurts to root cuttings of tropicals and tender perennials that will mature quickly in summer's heat and bloom with their parents. Taking cuttings of fresh growth again in late summer and fall is the best way to overwinter plants that grow too large to easily bring inside. Those original cuttings might stretch and become gangly through the winter but they will produce new growth in early spring ripe for taking a fresh round of cuttings to plant out in the garden.

The first step is to choose a rooting medium. Most of us have successfully rooted coleus and begonia cuttings in small glasses of water set on the windowsill. But water has a couple of drawbacks. Some plants will rot before they root. And because water doesn't offer new roots any resistance, rooted cuttings may take a while to adjust to growing in soil.

The ideal rooting medium will retain moisture but still drain well. It should also be coarse enough for oxygen to reach the buried stem, sterile, low in fertility, and supportive enough to keep the cuttings from falling over. The best options, used singly or in combination, are perlite (a crispy white volcanic glass capable of holding ten times its weight in water), and

vermiculite (an expanded mica that also holds a lot of water without becoming waterlogged), both of which are lightweight, perfect support for the delicate root systems of most perennials. Coarse sand, peat moss, or soilless potting mix may also be used but are less ideal. (Sand is dense, better suited for shrub and tree cuttings, and it can be difficult to regulate the moisture content in peat moss and potting soil.)

Professional propagators use a shaded cutting bench filled with their preferred medium and rigged with bottom heat and a system that automatically mists the cuttings when the medium begins to go dry. The rest of us can use a homemade Forsythe pot, which doesn't require complicated plumbing and works just as well. With this method, one container (preferably plastic) holds the medium and cuttings as they root, while a smaller porous terracotta pot sits in the center of the first container and gradually and evenly seeps water to the cuttings. A clear plastic bag tented over the top keeps the humidity level high, which helps prevent wilting.

Taking tip cuttings

In most plants, the versatile cells that wait for hormonal direction before growing into whatever the plant needs—be it shoots, roots, or leaves—reside in leaf nodes along the stem, at the very tips of a plant's freshest growth. Convince those cells to make roots by exposing and burying them.

Choosing the tips

Early morning, before the leaves have transpired the day's water away, look for new growth and critique it like Goldilocks. If the stem is floppy and weak, it's too soft. If it's stiff and woody, it's too hard. If it's flexible and green, it's just right. Try to find tips that haven't yet produced a flower bud. That is especially difficult in late summer, when plants are extra busy producing flowers from every tip. Look for non-flowering new growth at the base of the plant or from lower leaf axils.

If a plant hasn't produced cutting-worthy growth by the start of the school season, try pruning a few of the plant's stems by half (or to the ground) to trigger a fresh flush that will be ready for cutting in two to four weeks. Otherwise settle for tips with the smallest undeveloped buds. Remove growing tips below at least two sets of leaves (three to be safe). If you can't immediately

MAKE A FORSYTHE POT

MATERIALS

1 clean gallon-sized plastic nursery pot and saucer
1 sheet of paper towel or window screen (sized to cover the drainage holes of the plastic pot)
Perlite or vermiculite
1 unglazed terracotta pot (4-inch diameter) with rubber stopper or cork

STEPS

1. Cover the drainage holes of the plastic pot with the paper towel or window screen. Then fill the pot almost to the top with the perlite or vermiculite medium.
2. Plug the drainage hole of the terracotta pot with the stopper or cork. Place the terracotta pot into the center of the medium and push it down so that it sits flush with the top of the plastic pot.
3. Run water through the medium and then fill the terracotta reservoir with water. The Forsythe pot is now ready for your tip or leaf cuttings.

A Forsythe pot with an assortment of cuttings taking root.

prepare the cuttings for sticking in rooting medium, place them in a jar of water or wrap them in a wet paper towel inside a plastic baggie to prevent wilting.

Prepping the tips

To prepare cuttings, you will need to make a few cuts with a clean sharp knife, scalpel, or razor blade. Make the first cut 1/4 to 1/2 inch below the second or third set of leaves, then cut the lowest set of leaves off at the stem, taking care to not damage the stem. New roots will form from these cells at the leaf node and

the stem end. Cut the remaining leaves in half to keep the cutting from transpiring more water than the stem can draw, and remove any flower buds to help divert energy to root production instead.

Some plants are sufficiently hormonal on their own but giving them a little extra incentive with rooting hormone won't hurt. You can purchase rooting hormone in powdered form, with and without fungicide —choose the one with—or as a gel. Dip the end of the stem in rooting hormone and tap off the excess. (Rather than dipping straight into the container, fill a small dish as you need it—this will prevent possible contamination.)

You can also make your own rooting hormone using willow (*Salix*) twigs, which happen to be

Finding a decent tip for cutting on a blue anise sage (*Salvia guaranitica*).

An African blue basil (*Ocimum* 'African Blue') tip cutting before and after preparing it for sticking.

excessively hormonal and full of infection-fighting salicylic acid. The process is simple. Cut first-year growth from any willow, remove the leaves, and recut the twigs into 1-inch sections. Place them in a bowl, cover with boiling water, and let them stand overnight. In the morning, strain out the twigs and refrigerate the water, which should remain useful for up to two months. Let your cuttings stand in the willow water for a few hours before sticking them in the medium.

Ready for rooting

Use a pencil or chopstick as a dibble to poke holes in the rooting medium of the Forsythe pot. (The holes should be just deep and wide enough to insert your cuttings.) The bottom of the cutting should contact the medium with the cut leaf node under the surface. Snug the cuttings in so they stand upright and allow for airspace between them. Cover the pot with a clear plastic bag, supporting the bag with a few pencils or chopsticks to keep it from collapsing onto the cuttings.

Place the pot in a warm, bright spot out of direct sunlight. Check periodically to see if the terracotta pot needs to be refilled with water; at the same time, tug the cuttings gently to determine if they have rooted. If they resist, they're ready. If they still feel loose, they need more time (two to four weeks should do

A Forsythe pot full of cuttings and tented with a plastic bag to keep the moisture level high.

the trick). Once cuttings have rooted, scoop them out gently and pot them up—there's no need to remove any medium that stays attached to the roots. When you are finished, top up your Forsythe pot and start all over again. Note that vermiculite breaks down much faster than perlite so it may need to be replaced more often.

Taking leaf cuttings

Certain frost-tender keepers (begonias, echeveria, graptopetalum, and kalanchoe, for example) may be propagated from their leaves as well as stems. Leaf cuttings not only root, they generate a plantlet, a whole new tiny plant.

To propagate any plant whose leaves are attached by a petiole (fleshy stem): cut off a leaf, keeping an inch or so of its petiole, then dip the end in rooting hormone, shake off the excess, and stick the leaf upright in the rooting medium. If the leaf is large, cut off the top half to reduce transpiration. Leaf cuttings may take a month or two to form roots and a plantlet at the base of the petiole.

To propagate the leaves of succulents, snap them off at the stem and lay them on their side or stand them upright in the soil or medium. Plantlets will form, usually within a month, from the broken end. Dusting with rooting hormone powder is optional.

A fallen leaf from *Graptoveria* 'Fred Ives' (a cross of echeveria and graptopetalum) forming roots and a plantlet.

OVERWINTERING: IN FROM THE COLD

The sliding scale of effort involved in keeping tender plants alive over the winter ranges from really easy to not difficult at all. What you'll be capable of depends on how much you can lift without injury, how much control you have over the indoor climate, and how much space is available. After that, all you need to do is monitor your plants' needs, mostly for water.

During the winter, you can store and enjoy plants in three kinds of spaces. Some plants prefer to keep growing, and even blooming, indoors on warm windowsills. More will be happy to slow down to a standstill in a space that is bright and chilly but above freezing, such as a greenhouse, cold frame, or enclosed porch. And others will willingly go dormant in cool, dark storage. Each space and the plants overwintering in it will require different timing (for coming inside and going back out again in spring) and different levels of attention through the winter.

Overwintering on the warm windowsill

The same temperature range that keeps exiled gardeners comfortable and the pipes from freezing (high 50s to 60s F at night into the 60s and 70s F during the day) is also ideal for growing cuttings and for overwintering tropical plants, otherwise known, at least while they're indoors, as houseplants.

Welcoming plants into living spaces, particularly over the winter when we miss the garden madly, offers a variety of benefits. Walk into a plant-filled room and your heart rate actually lowers: plants reduce stress. Houseplants have also been proven to filter gaseous toxins known as Volatile Organic Compounds (VOCs) out of the air we breathe. As plants purify our air they take in carbon dioxide and emit oxygen, which reduces the likelihood of headaches and improves our sleep. And according to studies (and personal experience, as I stare deeply at a begonia for just the right words), plants inspire creativity. Indoor plants do require watering and regular attention but that is part of their charm. Taking care of a living thing can alleviate symptoms of depression, the blues, and cabin fever.

Plants also raise indoor humidity levels, staving off cold symptoms such as sniffly noses and coughing. Most houses, particularly when the heat is on, are very dry, usually below 30 percent humidity. Plants and people both prefer more humid conditions: 40 percent for cacti and succulents, 50 to 60 percent for the rest of us. The more plants that are transpiring water vapor from their leaves, the higher the moisture level

Looking down into the warm "Long House" at Logee's Greenhouses in Danielson, Connecticut.

in the air. Placing indoor plants on humidity trays will further increase air moisture. These trays, or saucers, should be 1 or 2 inches deep, filled with water and enough pebbles to keep the pots from sitting directly in the water. As the water evaporates, the humidity level will rise around your plants.

Locating light

Even in houses with covetable natural light, daylight is elusive during the winter. The sun, low on the horizon, weakens in intensity, and glass lets in less light than you might think. Add to that, most of us who desire privacy have also covered our windows either with foundation shrubs or curtains.

Start by taking an inventory of shadows. If you or the cat lying in a sunbeam cast a sharp shadow for a few hours a day, you've got decent light. The farther you move away, even from your brightest window, the darker it gets, the more diffuse the shadows. You might still be able to read the fine print on a sunny day but a sun-loving plant will have to stretch toward the window in order to photosynthesize the sun's energy. Use your findings to evaluate available windowsill real estate in your house and place your plants wherever their specific light requirements are most likely to be met. Be sure to position all sun-loving plants as close to the glass as possible.

- **South-facing** windows provide the brightest overall exposure through the winter (in the Northern hemisphere) so reserve those windowsills for sun-loving succulents, geraniums, and citrus.
- **West-facing** windows offer a warm afternoon glow. This is a fine second choice for tropical plants like hibiscus and glory bush.

LEFT A window full of begonias, a fig, hoya, and orchids raise the humidity level in my studio. OPPOSITE A Meyer lemon, scented geranium, and begonia share a sunny west-facing corner.

A tillandsia and a few rabbit's foot ferns thrive in the light and humidity of an east-facing windowsill above the kitchen sink.

- **East-facing** windows, with their morning sun, give a gentle boost to cuttings and seedlings.
- **North-facing** windows deliver diffuse light that will be fine for most ferns and understory plants like aspidistra and farfugium. But when the sun is distant and weak even shade-loving plants like these would do well in an east-facing window, or away from the windows in a bright room with southern or western exposure.

Time it right: coming in for winter

The timing of the move inside can mean the difference between life and death. In fall, scan the weather forecasts for frost warnings and play it safe. Start bringing your tropical plants inside as soon as night temperatures are forecast to dip into the mid-50s F. If temperatures plunge quickly in your area, plan ahead and give the plants destined for the living room a chance to acclimate by bringing them inside two weeks or so before you close windows and turn on the heat. Give potted plants their last dose of fertilizer in late summer. (Continue to feed winter bloomers every two weeks to a month until blooms fade.) Even though natural predators will generally help keep insect infestations to a minimum over summer outside, check your plants for hitchhikers, and wash them off if necessary before bringing them inside.

Winter watering

Judging the amount of water to give plants is probably the trickiest variable for most indoor gardeners. When getting to know your plants, think about where they grow wild. Plants from a rainforest floor will need to be kept evenly moist, which means the soil should never be allowed to dry out. But that doesn't mean they should sit constantly in a full dish of water; only plants from a bog habitat will tolerate that. Plants from climates with limited rainfall do better if their soil dries to the touch between watering. Their leaves may even be allowed to wilt, but then we have to drench them. And we have to pay attention to any seasonal watering requirements too. Many plants' dormant season is a dry one.

Plants send out distress signals when they need water but they will become stressed and unhealthy if wilting is the only cue you use. Instead, make a habit of checking their soil a few times a week. You'll see indicators by looking at the potting soil (it lightens in color as it dries) and sticking your finger in it (the soil will either feel cool and moist, or dry and dusty, to the touch). But the best way to test for soil dryness beyond the surface is to test its weight. If the pot and plant feel heavy, the soil is moist; if it feels light, it's dry.

Water plants in the morning so they can take advantage of the day's light to pull water up into their leaves through photosynthesis. Always water thoroughly enough that it runs out the drainage hole at the bottom of the pot. (This will encourage the roots to grow down rather than staying near the surface.) Allow your plants to sit in puddled saucers for a few hours to give the soil and roots a chance to absorb what's needed, then empty the excess. The warmer the temperature, outside or in, and the brighter the light, the more often plants will need to be watered. And vice versa: the cooler the temperature, the lower the light, the slower the growth, the less water is required.

Many plants have phototropic hormones in their stems that cause them to lean toward the sun, so rotate them a quarter turn every time you water to keep them balanced and standing straight.

Whenever you pot up plants, be sure to leave a watering well of at least half an inch between the soil and the pot's rim to prevent overflows and washouts.

Insect pests indoors

Even if we encourage insects in our garden we're unlikely to welcome them inside the house because they're messy eaters and they gross out the other members of our household. The most common houseplant pests are aphids, whitefly, scale, mealybug, and spider mite.

ABOVE LEFT Aphids on an African blue basil (*Ocimum* 'African Blue') cutting.
ABOVE RIGHT To control spider mite, which thrive in low humidity, and are evident when leaves become stippled and pale, hose plants off and place them in a humidity tray.

When plants are thriving and unstressed, adequately watered and groomed, devastating infestations are unlikely. So aim for health and keep your insecticidal arsenal as friendly as possible. If you can't dislodge insects with your fingers or a blast of water, try spraying with insecticidal soap or diluted dish soap (one small squeeze to a spray bottle full of water). Along with killing most insect pests on contact, this is also useful for washing dust and mold off of the leaves.

Other nontoxic insecticides include horticultural oil (a petroleum-based oil suspended in water), neem oil (which is pressed from the seeds of an Indian tree), and alcohol. Even nontoxic insecticides can damage some plants so always test your chosen remedy on a couple of leaves before dousing the whole plant. If the leaves shed, or look scorched or bruised, try something else. Keep your plants out of direct sun for a day or two after treatment and rinse them off to remove dead bugs and residual insecticide.

Time it right: spring fever

In late winter or early spring, plants begin to respond to the sun's climb in the sky, just as we do. The brighter light and warmer temperatures that entice us out into the garden also spur our houseplants to grow and increase their rate of transpiration. Do not abandon

INDOOR PLANT GROOMING

Gather a grooming kit—watering can, shears, a spray bottle of soapy water, a damp rag, and a dustpan and whiskbroom—so you can tidy as you go. Prune and sweep dead leaves and spent flowers into the tub. Squirt insect pests and use the rag to clean off their honeydew excreta. In the winter, I call this "gardening" and find it pretty gratifying.

RIGHT Salt deposits on the soil and pot indicate that I over-fertilized this fern.

them. They'll suddenly need to be watered more often. Early spring is also the time to start fertilizing again. Any plant destined to spend the summer in a container, especially those that flower or fruit heavily, will need to be fertilized regularly through the growing season to make up for the lack of nutrients available in potting soil and to replace what gets used up and washed out.

Give your plants a very dilute (about half a teaspoon to a gallon) dose of water-soluble fertilizer formulated for houseplants such as a standard NPK (nitrogen, phosphorus, potassium) ratio of 20-20-20, once every two weeks to a month, watered into soil

PLANT TOXICITY

Some children and pets will eat anything, and unfortunately, unless we're talking about Brussels sprouts, dietary adventurism isn't necessarily a good thing. Plants, like sharp tacks, have ingenious ways of protecting themselves from predators.

A lot of beautiful plants are toxic to eat and most of us have had poisonous plants in our garden forever and never had to rush anyone to the hospital. For a list of plants toxic to humans, visit the National Capital Poison Center (www.poison.org/prevent/plants.asp). Children are quick learners. Encourage them to garden with you and then watch them like a hawk. Call 1-800-222-1222 if they ever swallow anything they shouldn't.

Before trying to memorize the entire list of poisonous plants compiled by the ASPCA (www.aspca.org/pet-care/poison-control/plants/), and restricting your houseplant choices, observe your pets' habits and try behavior modification. Most cats, for instance, like to chew on grassy blades. Cabbage palm is on the do-not-eat list but they can chew papyrus to nubs and New Zealand flax to ribbons without risk of depression or internal bleeding. Even so, it's better to give cats their very-own dish of cat grass, which is usually a sweet mix of rye, oat, barley, and wheat grasses that germinates from seed within a week. If your cats are anything like mine, they'll go for that and ignore the rest. (Sow a fresh crop every two to three weeks.)

Dogs often chew anything and everything out of boredom and frustration but also will go for

Pigeon strikes a pose mid-snack.

grass-like plants when their stomachs are upset. If they need grass to settle their stomach, ask the cats to share. If you suspect your pet has been poisoned by ingesting a plant, call their vet immediately.

that is already moist. Plants in sunny windows or full-sun outside will need to be fed more often than those growing in lower light.

You might think that if a little is good, more is better: not so with fertilizer. Salts leached on the outside of terracotta pots or the surface of the soil is a sign of overdoing it. Scrape salty crusts off the soil, replace that soil if any roots have become exposed, and give your over-fertilized plant a good soaking to run the excess down the drain. And make your solution even more dilute next time. Keep track of your feedings in a calendar or garden notebook.

Also remember to pay extra-close attention to your plants after you have fertilized them and they are putting on succulent new growth. That is temptation enough for any herbivorous insect that might be able to find its way in, but spring's changes in temperature and humidity add to their stress making them easy prey. Don't let them be eaten alive.

Plants that spend the whole year in containers will indicate that they need to be repotted when they dry out daily, fail to thrive, or bust through their pot. Spring and early summer, before or as you move them outside is a fine time to tackle that task.

When outdoor temperatures rise into the mid-50s at night, begin to move your plants back outside. Even if they have been in sunny windows, let them acclimate to higher light levels by hardening them off in the shade for a week or two. Check for scorch marks after moving them into the sun and give them more time in the shade if necessary.

Overwintering in a bright and chilly space
It's Murphy's Law that the majority of tender plants we might want to winter over will thrive in the kind of environment most of us have very little of: a brightly sunlit space that warms gently during the day and is

chilly (35 to 60 degrees F) at night. What gardener wouldn't give up chocolate for a cool greenhouse in which to protect temperate zone evergreens like cuphea, felicia, rosemary, succulents, phormium. and farfugium?

A variety of keepers including phormium, colocasia, abutilon, geranium, and echeveria in my plantry.

In lieu of that dream greenhouse, which would likely be cost prohibitive to erect and maintain, consider using an enclosed porch (I call mine "the plantry") or attaching a cold frame to the south side of the house. A cold frame is simply a glass or poly-carbonate topped (and sometimes sided) box that sits on the ground or over a pit for extra insulation. Make it yourself from old window sashes—slope the top to shed snow and hinge it for easy venting—or buy one premade from any garden or greenhouse supply company. Whether your ersatz greenhouse is an enclosed porch like mine or a cold frame, use a portable heater plugged into a timer to keep your plants from freezing on cold nights.

Another option, if your house's thermostat has settings for more than one zone, is to populate your brightest room with plants and turn the heat down low, to 55 degrees F or lower, at night. Supplement any daylight that falls across that room with grow-lights. A combination of one cool-white and one full-spectrum fluorescent tube in a standard double-chan-neled fixture fitted with a reflector, will sufficiently cover the wavelengths necessary for plants' health. Hang it above a wide shelf fitted with a humidity tray. Plug the fixture into a timer that will turn it off only after your plants have received twelve to sixteen hours of light and adjust the lamp to keep it 8 to 12 inches above the tips of your plants. With a bank of grow-lights, you can turn even a corner of the basement or garage into a cool winter "greenhouse."

Time it right: coming in for winter

Plants destined to spend the winter in bright, chilly storage can stand to stay outside until just before a killing frost. Keep your eye on the forecast and don't let them get nipped. If your area tends to get

A frosted morning in Blithewold's Idea Garden.

premature light frosts interspersed with summery weather that would otherwise extend the garden season, cover frost-tender plants with a sheet on cold nights to enjoy them outside as long as possible. As with plants that come into the house's living spaces, stop fertilizing potted plants in late summer. Make it easier on yourself by digging and potting plants up in stages rather than all at once the day before a forecast frost warning. Cut large plants back by at least a third to help prevent transplant shock and wilting, and so they'll take up less space, and be easier to move.

Winter care

Plants that are kept cold and barely growing won't need quite as much attention as those growing in the warmth of the house. As a rule, water temperate-zone perennials and shrubs just before their soil dries completely. Allow succulents and desert plants to go dry; depending on how cold the space is, they may only need to be drenched once every two weeks to a month. Groom dead leaves and give plants a quarter turn every week or two to keep them standing straight.

If mold begins to grow, cut affected parts back to healthy stems, give plants more space, and make sure saucers are empty. Turn a small fan on low to help circulate the air.

Keep an eye out for insect pests even though cold temperatures tend to slow infestations. Control insects as you would with plants growing in the house.

Time it right: spring fever

In late winter or early spring, cut herbaceous perennials and shrubs back again by half or to the lowest set of buds. New growth will form that, in four to eight weeks' time, will be perfect for taking cuttings. Begin to fertilize again in early spring as new growth emerges.

Just as inside the house, plants will respond vigorously to the changes in temperature and day length. Your "greenhouse" will heat up during the day and may need to be opened and cooled to keep plants from

LEFT Geraniums (*Pelargonium*) growing in a sunny barn "orangerie."

PUSH THE ZONE OUTSIDE

If you don't have enough room inside for all of your favorite tender plants, or if you've taken all the cuttings you want, you have nothing to lose by leaving some plants in the ground. Occasionally we are dealt an unseasonably warm winter or an insulating blanket of snow. Or, if we take advantage of garden microclimates such as south-facing stone walls and foundations that hold and radiate extra warmth during the winter, we might just get lucky. Every gardener has at least one story about a surprising survivor and can tell you that nothing is more thrilling than seeing a salvia or dahlia return from the dead. Take your chances with plants at the edge of your own hardiness zone.

To give marginally hardy plants a fighting chance, leave their stems standing to protect their crown and to avoid stimulating new growth too tender to survive a cold snap. Cover their root zone with shredded leaves, bark mulch, or leftover holiday greens. In spring, pull any matted mulch and heavy greens away from the crown of the plant. Shredded leaves, being lighter in texture, may be left longer as protection. Cut stems back in late spring and do a little probing to check for signs of life but don't expect to see any new shoots until the soil warms.

Placing shredded leaf protection around the crown of *Agastache* 'Heatwave'.

becoming stressed by heat and dryness, and susceptible to predation. Water daily to weekly in spring and remember to close the windows, doors, or vents again on cold nights.

As outside temperatures warm above freezing at night, move the hardiest plants back outside. Harden them off in the shade for a week or two before moving them gradually into more sun. Week-by-week, as weather permits, continue moving the plants outside until all have found their places in the garden.

Overwintering in a dark and cool space

Closets, storage crates, basements, crawl spaces, garages, or any place that can be kept dark and above freezing, are ideal for storing tuberous rooted and herbaceous perennials, and deciduous shrubs and trees, which lose their leaves in their native climate and expect to get a real rest between growing seasons. The temperature should hover between 35 and 60 degrees F; the light level should be dim to pitch black, day and night.

Every gardener's dark storage space is different: a storage method that results in moldy rot for me, might foster plump, healthy root tissue for you. Use a humidity meter to chart moisture levels. In dry spaces, potted plants will need to be watered more often, whereas in damp spaces, you'll have to watch for signs of mold

Dahlia 'Baronesse' touched by frost.

and rot. The humidity level will also affect storage. When dry, try storing plants in open plastic bags or in boxes barely covered with dampened potting mix or peat moss; when damp, pack bareroot tubers and corms loosely in open bins, wrapped in newspaper, and in paper bags rather than plastic. Dusting with fungicide is optional. Experiment.

Time it right: coming in for winter

Plants destined for dark storage should be hit by frost before coming inside—a cold zap is the best way to shut down bloom production and trigger dormancy. Stop fertilizing potted plants in late summer or early fall and water them less frequently, allowing growth to slow as the temperatures dip. Also make sure you have labeled your plants before frost blackens their stems and blooms.

Unless an arctic freeze is forecast, wait a couple of days to two weeks after the first frost before digging plants out of the garden. This will give their roots a chance to get the message and gather resources for the winter. (Dahlia tubers swell with carbohydrates and water as temperatures plunge.)

Plants with tuberous roots or corms (such as dahlia, canna, four o'clocks, and gladiolus) may be stored barerooted. Use a digging fork to gently lift them out of the ground. Cut stems down to 3 to 6 inches, remove any soil from around the roots and dry them off in the sun upside-down for a day or two before storing them. Plants with fibrous roots (such as salvia, lemon verbena, fuchsia, and palm grass) should be stored potted up. Use a spade to dig them out of the ground, keeping plenty of soil around the roots. Cut their stems down as well, by at least a third to make moving them inside easier. Water them in well after potting up.

Dahlia tubers brought up from storage already beginning to sprout.

Winter care

Out of sight out of mind? Plants overwintering in dark storage need very little attention but try not to forget about them completely: check them at least once a month.

If bareooted plants begin to shrivel, mist tubers or dampen packing material. Air them out if you see

Potting up dahlia tubers.

signs of mold, and promptly remove any mushy or rotten bits.

Potted plants should be kept "just moist," meaning they should be watered only sparingly before the soil becomes bone-dry. The darker and damper the space, the less frequently they will require watering and vice versa. Some plants, like tuberous begonia and pineapple lily won't need any water at all. Tip those pots on their side as a reminder.

Time it right: spring fever

As light levels increase in spring, so do ambient temperatures and even plants that have been dormant in the dark will notice. Begin watering potted plants if they are noticeably dry, or as soon as they show signs of growing. If it has been a wet spring, tubers might need to be aired out to keep them plump and firm. If the spring is dry, mist packing material to keep roots from desiccating. But don't be overly worried if the tubers shrivel this late in the game. Sometimes they will still sprout when you plant them and you've got nothing to lose by trying.

If you have room in your makeshift greenhouse (you should, after moving the hardiest plants out), bring your dormant plants into the light to give them a head start of about a month before planting them outside. It is a good idea to pot up tubers at this point too. This will help them bloom sooner, and visibly growing plants will be easier to work around after planting them in the garden. If you decide to plant tubers straight into the ground, wait until after your average last frost date, when the soil is warm, and mark the sites well. It usually takes two or three weeks for their shoots to emerge.

Fuchsia, brugmansia, four o'clocks, palm grass, begonias, and dahlias spending the winter in my cellar.

50 COME-BACK KEEPERS

An outstanding display of foliage and flowers is worth a pretty penny, but it will always be easier to open your wallet for plants that promise to stick around. Bank on these fifty frost-tender favorites and experiment with anything else you bring through the garden gate. Give in to exciting temptations available locally as well as a whole wild world of options available from mail-order sources. Borrow exotic contrasts from Asia and Africa, super-saturated late-summer colors from Central and South America, and succulent sculpture from the American Southwest. Then spend only time, and spare some space to keep them growing to embellish your garden for seasons to come.

Notice that in many instances, there is more than one way to overwinter a keeper. Some will be as happy to go dormant in dark storage as they would slowing to a standstill on a chilly, bright porch. Many tolerate a range of temperatures and light levels and can be asked to fill (and decorate) any windowsill vacancy. A few might even make it staying put out in the garden. No doubt you'll find, with all of the possibilities and permutations, that you have more room for frost-tender plants—in your budget and garden—than you thought.

Go a step further and propagate frost-tender plants as soon as you get them home even if the tag reads "propagation prohibited" (that only means you if selling plants is your business). By making the most of these plants' natural vigor you'll be able to fill your garden with beauties guaranteed to keep your garden blooming, and your interest piqued, well into fall. Then share your enthusiasm with friends, enjoy their compliments, and congratulate yourself for being able to take a year-long garden season, outdoors and in, for granted.

OPPOSITE Flowering maple (variegated *Abutilon pictum* 'Gold Dust' in the foreground with *A.* ×*hybridum* 'Red Monarch') and other tender-perennial temptations at Avant Gardens.

Abutilon
FLOWERING MAPLE, PARLOR MAPLE

Abutilon 'Kristen's Pink'

Shrub | Zones 8 to 10

DESCRIPTION Small hibiscus-like flowers appear along branches of palmate, moleskin-soft leaves. Where hardy, these plants can reach heights and widths of 10 ft. or more but they can be pinched while in active growth to keep them from getting leggy, and pruned back by a third each year in early spring to control their size in containers. Place them at the top of the plant stand where you can look up their high-waisted ballet tutu–blooms as they open.

FINE PRINT Prefers full sun and moist soil. To keep abutilon flowering year-round, provide plenty of light and fertilize every two weeks in spring and summer, and once per month fall and winter. Propagate by tip cuttings anytime. Overwinter in chilly or warm conditions with southern or western exposure; water when dry; use a humidity tray to prevent spider mite; watch for aphids and whitefly.

Acalypha wilkesiana
JACOB'S COAT, COPPER LEAF

Acalypha wilkesiana 'Devappa'

Shrub | Zones 10 to 11

DESCRIPTION Broad, hand-sized, calico foliage adorns woody branches capable of growing 6 ft. tall. Sparklingly fuzzy flower spikes are considered "insignificant" but I think they are cool, especially when backlit by late-summer sun. Plant with dahlias, salvias, mountain mint, and elephant's ear in a mixed and modern garden.

FINE PRINT Prefers full sun to partial shade, and moist soil. Pinch top growth to encourage branching and shape plants as needed. Propagate by tip cuttings in late summer. Overwinter in warm conditions with southern or western exposure; keep soil moist.

Aeonium arboreum

HOUSELEEK TREE, TREE ANEMONE

Aeonium arboreum 'Atropurpureum'

Perennial or shrub | Zones 9 to 15

DESCRIPTION Rosettes of strappy green to burgundy leaves vary in diameter from 3 to 8 in. and rise to 3 ft. or more on curvy naked stems and branches. Pyramidal clusters of bright yellow vanilla-scented stars hover above in winter. Give this oddity its own container and surround it with a crazy-quilt pattern of burgundy or chartreuse coleus. The cultivar 'Zwartkop' has lustrous burgundy-black foliage and needs more sun.

FINE PRINT Prefers partial shade, and dry, well-drained soil. Propagate by cutting off a rosette where the stem is still green; dust the stem end with rooting hormone and stick in medium. (New rosettes will also form on the decapitated stem.) Overwinter in chilly or warm conditions with eastern or western exposure; water when dry.

Agapanthus africanus

LILY OF THE NILE

Agapanthus africanus

Perennial | Zones 9 to 10

DESCRIPTION Airy bobbles of purplish blue trumpets sway on 2- to 3-ft. leafless stems over strappy foliage in mid to late summer. The deep blue–flowered cultivar 'Midnight Blue' stands 1½ to 2 ft. tall and is hardy in zones 7 to 9, where summers are moist and winters dry. Plant them in tight quarters against foundations, curbs and rock outcrops, or in containers—they bloom best when root-bound.

FINE PRINT Prefers full sun, and moist, well-drained soil. Fertilize every two weeks starting in early spring until bloom cycle finishes. Propagate by dividing overgrown clumps in spring. (Let the soil dry completely before unpotting.) Overwinter in chilly conditions with eastern or southern exposure; water when dry and remove yellow leaves.

Agastache
HUMMINGBIRD MINT, SUNSET HYSSOP

Agastache mexicana 'Acapulco Orange' intermixed with asters (*Aster ×frikartii* 'Monch').

Perennial | Zones vary

DESCRIPTION Spires of luminous tubes with deeply tinted calyxes open from mid to late summer and attract hummingbirds better than a feeder. The 2- to 4-ft. tall whip-thin stems and gray-green foliage of this southwestern native wildflower are licorice scented. Plant wherever lavender thrives, underplanted with moss rose (*Portulaca grandiflora*) and sedums. *A. mexicana* 'Acapulco Orange' (zones 6 to 9) grows 2 ft. tall with orange flowers, while the hybrid 'Heatwave' (zones 5 to 10) glows in shades of fuchsia to Bazooka-style pink.

FINE PRINT Prefers full sun and well-drained soil. Drought tolerant once established. Propagate by tip cuttings in spring and late summer. Where marginally hardy, make sure winter drainage is sharp and mulch the crown; cut plants to the ground in spring. Cut plants back to 6 in. or less before potting and bringing inside. Overwinter in chilly conditions with eastern or southern exposure and good air circulation; water when dry.

Agave americana
CENTURY PLANT

Monocarpic succulent | Zones 9 to 11

DESCRIPTION Sculptural swirls of twisted, looping, and sharply barbed spears imprinted like fossils will eventually grow a 25-ft. tall flower spike and die. Meanwhile, endless offshoots or "pups" are produced around the base of the mother plant. This agave grows and spreads rapidly in the ground but tolerates confinement in pots. Plant it as a focal point in a dry garden with hummingbird mint, Mexican feather grass, and stonecrop or as a container garden conversation piece.

FINE PRINT Prefers full sun, and dry, well-drained soil. Cut off terminal spines to prevent eye injury. Propagate by separating and replanting offshoots. If hit by frost outside, hose off to prevent scarring. Overwinter in chilly or warm conditions with southern or western exposure; water when bone-dry.

Agave americana in an eclectic kitchen garden combination.

Aloysia triphylla
LEMON VERBENA, HERB LOUISA

An elderly *Aloysia triphylla* standard at Green Animals Topiary Garden in Portsmouth, Rhode Island.

Deciduous shrub | Zones 8 to 11

DESCRIPTION Pointed citrusy leaves—which are especially aromatic during midsummer flowering—are produced on gangly stems that can grow 10 ft. tall in subtropical climates. You can manage its size by harvesting the stems to make tea or potpourri. Tuck it into the herb garden behind the lavender and lemongrass or use it as a green screen on the deck. Over the years, its trunk and stems will become as gnarled as an old olive tree.

FINE PRINT Prefers full sun, and rich, well-drained soil. Propagate by tip cuttings in summer. Where marginally hardy, plant lemon verbena against a warm south-facing wall and mulch the root zone. Overwinter in chilly bright conditions or in dark storage, potted; water sparingly when dry; prune to lowest dormant buds in spring.

Asparagus densiflorus 'Myersii'
ASPARAGUS FERN, FOXTAIL FERN

Asparagus densiflorus 'Myersii'

Perennial | Zones 9 to 10

DESCRIPTION These ground-covering tuffets of bristly, lime-green, 2-ft. long tentacles look more like undersea creatures than a terrestrial garden filler. Invisible fragrant early-summer flowers are sometimes followed by studs of small shiny Christmas-red fruit. Use its aquatic contrast in flower arrangements (fronds last well in water) and alongside the shiny spotted leaves of *Farfugium japonicum* 'Aureomaculatum', variegated hosta, and *Heuchera* 'Caramel'. Or isolate it in a container to ease the transition from outdoors in and back out again.

FINE PRINT Prefers partial shade to shade, and moist soil. Propagate by division. Overwinter in warm conditions with eastern or northern exposure; water when dry.

Aspidistra elatior
CAST-IRON PLANT

Aspidistra elatior

Perennial | Zones 7 to 11

DESCRIPTION This classic Victorian-era houseplant earns its keep over winter by greening-up the darkest corners in which most other indoor plants would stretch unattractively. In summer it forms a spreading 3-ft. tall groundcover, making a glossy (or variegated or spotted) backdrop curtain for shade containers and corners planted with spotted deadnettle and variegated ribbon grass.

FINE PRINT Prefers partial shade to shade, and moist soil. As its name suggests, cast-iron plant is practically indestructible; propagate by division using a saw or soil knife to get through the crown. Where marginally hardy, plant against a warm south-facing wall and cover in mulch. Overwinter in chilly or warm conditions with eastern or northern exposure; water when dry.

Begonia
TUBEROUS BEGONIA

Begonia sutherlandii

Perennial | Zones vary

DESCRIPTION Tuberous begonias use their nonstop summer flowers to grab the attention of gardeners. The plants in the Million Kisses Series (zones 9 to 11), specifically developed to spill down the shaded side of hanging baskets, have cascades of blushing pink or red, elongated, four-petaled bellbottoms and can grow an astonishing 1 × 3 ft. tall and wide. Sutherland's begonia (*B. sutherlandii*; zones 8 to 12) makes a 6- to 12-in. mound with red-edged, grass-green, lopsided-heart leaves—the ideal backdrop for summer-long dots of sherbet-orange petals. Drape it over the sides of containers or the edge of a rock wall and pair it with shade-loving, complementary blue *Lobelia erinus*.

FINE PRINT Prefers morning sun or partial shade, and dry, well-drained soil. Propagate by division, or allow Sutherland's begonia to self-sow. Bring plants inside before frost and overwinter in chilly (low-light) conditions, or in dark storage, potted—either way, plants will die back to the roots. Withhold water until new growth emerges in spring.

Brugmansia
ANGEL'S TRUMPET

Brugmansia versicolor 'Frosty Pink'

Shrub | Zones 9 to 11

DESCRIPTION Although angel's trumpet grows quickly from a rooted cutting into a 4- to 12-ft. tall tree with large soft leaves, it won't flower for most of us until late summer. But its enormous dangles of night-scented cream, apricot, yellow, or pink trumpets are worth the wait. Let it knock your socks off on the deck or feature it in the ground with other stupendous tropicals like canna and amaranth.

FINE PRINT Prefers full sun to partial (afternoon) shade, and moist soil. Pinch tips to encourage branching and fertilize every two weeks to a month from spring until late summer. Propagate by tip cuttings in spring. Overwinter in in chilly conditions with southern exposure or dark storage, potted; keep soil just moist either way. Cut back to a low framework before bringing indoors (unless you have the space to enjoy any remaining flower buds) or just before it breaks dormancy in early spring.

CANNA

Canna 'Bengal Tiger'

Perennial | Zones 8 to 11

DESCRIPTION The flamboyant late-summer flowers attract hummingbirds, but most gardeners choose cannas for their stalks of multicolored, zebra-striped, or matte blue-green leaves that are shaped like kayak paddles. Plant tall varieties (some grow to 10 ft., but 4 to 6 ft. is more common) at the back of a riotous hot-colored border with dahlias and four o'clocks where they will be backlit by morning or afternoon sun.

FINE PRINT Prefers full sun and moist soil. Plant rhizomes 4 to 6 in. deep in the ground after last frost or start them in pots earlier. Deadhead to keep plants blooming. Propagate by dividing rhizomes. Overwinter in dark storage, bareroot and dry, wrapped in newspaper, in open bins or paper bags; mist with water if plants show signs of shriveling.

Citrus ×meyeri 'Meyer'
MEYER LEMON

Citrus ×meyeri 'Meyer'

Shrub | Zones 9 to 11

DESCRIPTION The fruit of this lemon–mandarin orange cross, ripe when it turns as yellow as yolk, is sweet-tart with a thin edible rind. Consult Alice Waters' cookbooks for recipes and enjoy the shrub's shiny deep green leaves, fragrant white flowers that open from purple-blushed buds, and its prolific summer display of ripening orbs on a widely branching framework that can reach 6 to 10 ft. tall. Use it as a focal point on the deck with shrub verbena and scented geranium.

FINE PRINT Prefers full sun and moist soil. Fertilize monthly, year-round, with an acidic fertilizer formulated for citrus. Propagate by tip cuttings in late summer. Overwinter in chilly or warm conditions with southern or western exposure; keep soil just moist. For best fruit production use a soft watercolor brush to hand-pollinate winter flowers indoors. Prune in early spring for shape and to maintain size.

Colocasia
ELEPHANT'S EAR, TARO

Colocasia esculenta 'Nancy's Revenge', not yet displaying its distinctive cream-splashed center.

Cormous perennial | Zones 8 to 10

DESCRIPTION Variations in the two hundred or so cultivars of *C. esculenta* include leaf color from chartreuse to blue-green to purple-black and sizes from tea cup to garage (I exaggerate, but only slightly). The largest leaves of *C. gigantea* can grow 5 ft. long and nearly as wide. Plant at pond edges or with New Zealand flax and pink porterweed to add temperate and tropical-zone stylishness to northern gardens.

FINE PRINT Prefers full sun to partial shade, and rich, moist to boggy soil. Propagate by dividing rhizomatous types during growth, or separating corm offsets before planting. Overwinter big plants in dark storage: store large tubers bareroot, otherwise leave in pots and withhold water until spring. Provide warm conditions and eastern exposure for your favorite small plants, and keep soil evenly moist.

Cordyline australis
CABBAGE PALM

Cordyline australis 'Torbay Dazzler'

Tree | Zones 10 to 11

DESCRIPTION Brilliant arrow-straight and slightly arched 1- to 3-ft. long deep pinkish burgundy or green blades spray up and out from the top of a single stem—a trunk, over time—to catch our attention like a bright idea. With cream and pink-tinged-green variegation, 'Torbay Dazzler' is a quintessential thriller for container combinations. It also looks outstanding tucked in a garden border as a ray of light among a cluster of African blue basil or spur flower.

FINE PRINT Prefers full sun to partial shade, and moist soil. Control vertical growth by cutting off the growing tip—to the pot if necessary—in mid spring. This will cause multiple branches to form at the cut and/or along the trunk. Propagate by rooting tips and sections of stem; maintain the polarity of the stem pieces, sticking them vertically in medium. Overwinter in chilly or warm conditions with eastern or southern exposure; water when dry.

Cosmos atrosanguineus
CHOCOLATE COSMOS

Cosmos atrosanguineus

Tuberous perennial | Zones 7 to 11

DESCRIPTION I like to think that I would grow this plant even if the flowers didn't smell like Snickers. But in mid to late summer, the open-faced maroon petals hovering on licorice-whip stems and surrounding dark-chocolate centers really are candy scented. Plant their loose, spreading stems in a pot of mint, or around Mexican feather grass and spurges (especially *Euphorbia* ×*martinii* 'Ascot Rainbow') for color contrast.

FINE PRINT Prefers full sun, and rich, moist soil. Deadhead to keep plants flowering. Propagate by dividing tubers. In marginally hardy gardens, plant where drainage is sharp through the winter and mulch the crown. Overwinter in dark storage: when potted, keep soil just moist; when bareroot (in plastic bags or wrapped in newspaper), check the small, delicate tubers at least once a month and mist with water if they show signs of shriveling.

Cuphea
CIGAR PLANT, BAT FLOWER

Cuphea 'David Verity'

Shrub | Zones vary

DESCRIPTION Out of the more than 250 species, the hybrid 'David Verity' (zones 8 to 10)—with a 2-ft. mass of glossy green leaves and 1-in. long burning-ember flowers from midsummer to frost—is among the hummingbirds' favorites. But sticky-leaved *C. llavea* (zones 9 to 12) cultivars have ruffled petals like Mickey Mouse ears, which makes them even more fantasia-tastic. The hybrid 'Ballistic' has conspicuous deep purple ears and a compact habit perfect for poking through the branches of golden-yellow *Spiraea thunbergii* 'Ogon'.

FINE PRINT Prefers full sun to partial shade, and moist soil. Propagate by tip cuttings in spring and late summer. Overwinter in chilly conditions with eastern or southern exposure; water when dry; watch for aphids and whitefly.

Cyperus papyrus
PAPYRUS, EGYPTIAN PAPER RUSH

Cyperus papyrus

Perennial | Zones 9 to 10

DESCRIPTION Spreading 6-ft. tall triangular stalks that can be splayed for making paper or used as a curtain between garden rooms are topped by fiber-optic globes spritzed with tiny brown flowers. If its height is unnecessary, grow the 2- to 3-ft. dwarf *C. prolifer* or umbrella grass (*C. involucratus*), whose flowers appear between an umbrella's skeleton of grassy blades instead. Plant any of these species in the pond with elephant's ear and umbrella plant or in a tub in the container garden.

FINE PRINT Prefers full sun to partial shade, and wet soil—grow in standing water (a full saucer) year-round. Cut stalks to the ground when they turn brown. Propagate by division. Overwinter in chilly or warm conditions with eastern, southern, or western exposure.

DAHLIA

Dahlia 'Pale Tiger'

Tuberous perennial | Zones 9 to 11

DESCRIPTION Bumblebee-seducing, pollen-centric flowers grow on glossy stems with deep green to bronze cut foliage and come in every possible petal color but true-blue. You'll also find a shape and size for every gardener's taste, be it a miniature front-of-the-border daisy, multi-petal waterlily, cheerleader pompom, or spidery cactus flower. Colors intensify as nights cool and they won't quit until frost. Plant them in any sunny garden with late-blooming salvias, cannas, and asters where they will steal the show from midsummer daylilies and phlox.

FINE PRINT Prefers full sun and rich, moist soil. Plant tubers in the ground 4- to 6-in. deep in early summer after the soil warms or start them earlier inside in pots, planted just below the soil's surface. Propagate by separating tubers in spring before planting (each tuber should have a visible growing point or "eye") or by tip cuttings as new growth appears after planting. Deadhead for continuous bloom and best looks and use stakes to support tall varieties. Overwinter in dark storage, bareroot, in paper bags, open plastic bags, or wrapped in newspaper; mist with water if tubers show signs of shriveling.

Dicliptera sericea, syn. *D. suberecta*
URUGUAYAN FIRECRACKER PLANT

Dicliptera sericea

Perennial | Zones 13 to 15

DESCRIPTION The silver-green velvet covering the angular 1- to 2-ft. stems and the kitten's-ear leaves makes this plant a truly tactile treat, while midsummer to frost, firecracker-orange tubular hummingbird-feeder flowers are visually magnetic. Plant it in a stroke-able combination with peppermint-scented geranium and silver sage (*Salvia argentea*), or show it off against purple-leaved shiso and coleus.

FINE PRINT Prefers full sun to partial shade, and moist soil. Cut plants back to low leaf-sets in fall and again in spring. Propagate by tip cuttings in spring and early fall. Large plants grow from small root systems making them easy to dig out and pot up in fall. Overwinter in chilly conditions with southern or western exposure; keep soil just moist.

ECHEVERIA

Echeveria elegans

Succulent perennial | Zones vary from 10 to 15

DESCRIPTION At least 150 species—all native to the semi-deserts of southwestern United States, Central America, and South America—are available to choose from in this genus' jewelry box. Almost all have a distinctive hens-and-chicks–like rosette of fleshy or fuzzy, ruffled, spoon-shaped or curled-tongue foliage in a range of hues from concrete gray and celadon to red-edged lavender and burgundy. Star-burst flowers on nearly naked curled 12-in. stems hang on for weeks during the summer. Plant echeveria along the gardens fringes where drainage is sharp or in containers either by themselves or with other succulents and herbs that thrive in sun and sandy soil.

FINE PRINT Prefers full sun, and dry, well-drained soil. Some species produce an endless supply of offshoots while others are slower to spawn, but all can be propagated any time of the year by leaf cuttings or by rooting entire rosettes. Overwinter in chilly or warm conditions with southern or western exposure; provide low humidity and water when dry.

Eucomis comosa
PINEAPPLE LILY

Eucomis comosa 'Sparkling Burgundy'

Bulbous perennial | Zones 7 to 11

DESCRIPTION Columns of pale greenish white flowers crowned with leafy capitals, looking just like slender versions of their namesake fruit, rise 2-ft. tall in midsummer from clumps of wide strappy leaves. The cultivar 'Sparkling Burgundy' displays pink flowers on red stems and leaves that shift from deep burgundy to green and back again as the flowers fade. Plant pineapple lilies as exclamation points in containers or in the front row with plumbago and shiso.

FINE PRINT Prefers full sun and moist soil. Plant bulbs 6 in. deep in the ground in early summer as soil warms or just below the surface in pots. In marginally hardy gardens, plant where drainage is sharp enough to prevent rot. Propagate by separating offshoot bulbs in spring. Overwinter potted plants, which will die back completely, in chilly (low-light) conditions or in dark storage; do not water.

Euphorbia tirucalli 'Sticks on Fire'
PENCIL CACTUS

Euphorbia tirucalli 'Sticks on Fire' stands tall in a rainbow assortment of succulents at Avant Gardens.

Tree-like succulent | Zones 13 to 15

DESCRIPTION Glowing in shades from reddish coral to yellow, the densely forked, practically leafless, tubular pencil-thin twigs look as if they would be more at home in a reef than a dry stony slope. While the straight green species grows chaotically lanky, 'Sticks on Fire', which lacks the chlorophyll required for rapid growth, is more compact—potentially reaching 4 to 8 ft. as opposed to 25 ft.—and more upright. Bring out its colors by surrounding it with a tidal pool of blue-green echeveria.

FINE PRINT Prefers full sun, low humidity, and dry, well-drained soil. Like all euphorbias, 'Sticks on Fire' bleeds a caustic sap that can cause contact dermatitis and even blindness, so for goodness sake, do not touch your eyes after touching it. Propagate by tip cuttings anytime, letting the cut ends dry and form a callus before sticking in rooting medium. Overwinter in chilly or warm conditions with southern or western exposure; water when dry.

Farfugium japonicum
LIGULARIA, LEOPARD PLANT

Perennial | Zones 7 to 10

DESCRIPTION In mid to late fall, *F. japonicum* 'Aureomaculatum' sends 2- to 3-ft. tall deely-boppers of yellow daisies up from 12- to 18-in. clumps of shiny, deep green and yellow-speckled lilypad leaves. Contrast their circus display with hakonechloa, asparagus fern, or yellow-leaved St. John's wort (*Hypericum calycinum* 'Brigadoon'). With its 12-in. wide glossy green leaves on 2-ft. stalks, *F. japonicum* var. *giganteum* is more like an elephant in the garden than a leopard; it is ideal for traffic-stopping container displays.

FINE PRINT Prefers partial shade and moist soil. It will wilt during drought but is surprisingly resilient. Propagate by division. Where marginally hardy, plant against a south-facing wall protected from winter wind and mulch the crown. Overwinter in chilly or warm conditions with any exposure; keep soil moist.

Farfugium japonicum var. *giganteum* grows in a 30-in. pot with iresine, fuchsia, lobelia, and begonias.

Felicia amelloides
BLUE DAISY, BLUE MARGUERITE

Felicia amelloides 'Variegata'

Perennial | Zones 9 to 11

DESCRIPTION A profusion of sky-blue yellow-eyed daisies sit atop sprawling 12-in. mounds of wiry stems and tiny leathery leaves. Blooming slows as the humidity rises. The cultivar 'Variegata' is a great choice for gardeners who suffer muggy summers because even without flowers, its white and deep green foliage is bright enough to sparkle against chartreuse licorice vine (*Helichrysum petiolare* 'Limelight'). Burgundy-bronze foliage, like *Uncinia uncinata* 'Rubra' or 'Sedona' coleus, would bring out the cerulean in the early- and late-season flowers.

FINE PRINT Prefers full sun and moist soil. Pinch to encourage bushier growth. Propagate by tip cuttings in spring. Cut it back by a third to half when potting up and again in spring. Overwinter in chilly conditions with southern or western exposure; water when dry (but before the leaves wilt).

Ficus carica
COMMON FIG

Ficus carica 'Brown Turkey'

Small tree or shrub | Zones 8 to 10

DESCRIPTION Large, lobed, gray-green leaves decorate sculptural branches interspersed along the previous season's new growth with fleshy knobs of enclosed flowers that are, in fact, a sweet and sensual treat. 'Brown Turkey' and 'Chicago Hardy' are reliably hardy above zone 6 and capable of growing 15 to 25 ft. tall when planted in the ground. 'Petite Negra' is less hardy (to zone 8) but only grows 2 to 3 ft. tall in a container.

FINE PRINT Prefers full sun to partial shade, moist soil, and protection from wind. Propagate by tip cuttings in spring and prune after harvesting. Where marginally hardy, plant against a warm south-facing wall and peg branches to the ground for burial under an insulating blanket of shredded leaves. Overwinter potted plants in chilly conditions (any exposure) or in dark storage—either way they will drop their leaves and go dormant; keep soil just moist.

Ficus deltoidea
MISTLETOE FIG

Ficus deltoidea

Shrub | Zones 10 to 15

DESCRIPTION Slender woody branches arch, bend, and drape a collection of 2-in., pin-pricked, deep green teardrops with a pale reverse, along with yellow to orange pea-sized figlets. A favorite houseplant for low light, it also makes a textural container garden companion for hakonechloa, heuchera, fuchsia, and farfugium.

FINE PRINT Prefers bright light to partial shade, humidity, and moist soil. Shrubs can grow like trees to 15 ft. or more but may be pruned any time and even shaped and restricted like bonsai in containers. Propagate by tip cuttings in spring. Overwinter in warm conditions with any exposure; place on a humidity tray and keep soil evenly moist (but don't let it sit in water).

FUCHSIA

Fuchsia 'Gartenmeister Bonstedt'

Shrubs and perennials | Zones vary

DESCRIPTION So-called hardy fuchsias are just tender enough for most of us to have to make room for them inside. Grow the 1- to 3-ft. tall, regimentally upright 'Gartenmeister Bonstedt' (zones 9 to 10) for its army-green purple backed leaves and clusters of red bugles. Or *F. magellanica* var. *gracilis* 'Aurea' (zones 8 to 10) for its gaudy curtains of red-stemmed yellow leaves and pink-purple flowers. Plant their colors and hummingbird magnetism among the hostas or in foliage-heavy shade containers with farfugium and ferns.

FINE PRINT Prefers morning sun and afternoon shade, and rich, moist, well-drained soil. Deadheading is unnecessary but fertilization every two weeks to a month during summer is recommended especially for potted fuchsias. Propagate by tip cuttings in early and late summer. Overwinter potted plants in chilly conditions with southern or western exposure (keep soil evenly moist), or dormant in dark storage (water sparingly to keep soil just moist). Cut the stems back to the lowest visible buds in spring.

GLADIOLUS

Gladiolus murielae and tall verbena.

Cormous perennial | Zones 6 to 10

DESCRIPTION In high summer, when the garden is beginning to look beat by the heat, gladiolus offers spring-fresh blades rising 3 to 5 ft. tall with zigzagging spears of bottom-to-top opening butterfly wings. The single-sided stems curve and occasionally lean like drunks so grow them between crutches of plants like anise hyssop and summer phlox. *G. murielae* (zones 7 to 10), also known as acidanthera, has delicate foliage and 2- to 3-ft. tall stems accommodating up to a dozen nodding and highly fragrant white stars with burgundy centers.

FINE PRINT Prefers full sun and well-drained soil. Propagate by separating new corms from old (discard the old). Plant after last frost in two-week successions for a longer mid- to late-summer display. Wait at least six weeks after flowering to dig corms and cut stems to 2 in. before bringing inside. Overwinter in dark storage, completely dry, bareroot in paper or mesh bags.

Hibiscus rosa-sinensis
CHINESE HIBISCUS

Hibiscus rosa-sinensis hybrid

Shrub | Zones 9 to 11

DESCRIPTION Chinese hibiscus is the quintessential tropical flower. It has a wide ruff of show-off petals with a projecting boss of hummingbird- and butterfly-seducing flower parts that open in succession (every day or two) over the summer and intermittently through the winter on a stiff and upright woody, glossy green shrub. You'll earn bragging rights whenever it's in full flower: place it by the front door or the best spot on the deck. Pair Chinese hibiscus with brugmansia, canna, and palm grass as a reminder of your last trip to paradise.

FINE PRINT Prefers full sun, and rich, moist soil. Propagate by tip cuttings in spring and early summer. Fertilize every two weeks during summer to keep blooms coming. Cut back by a third to half before bringing inside, even if it is still flowering. Overwinter in warmish conditions (55 to 70 degrees F) with southern or western exposure; water when dry; watch for aphids, whitefly, mealybug, and scale.

KALANCHOE

Kalanchoe tomentosa

Succulent perennial | Zones 11 to 15

DESCRIPTION Gardeners can choose from more than one hundred upright and shrubby or dangly species, although I think it would be impossible to pick just one. Options include the nodding, flour-dusted, pink-flowered *K. pumila*; the upright, softly flocked, brown-tipped panda plant (*K. tomentosa*); and the stupendously prolific devil's backbone (*K. daigremontiana*), which arrays tiny gray plantlets around the edges of its pointed seafoam-green leaves. Use kalanchoe to extend your succulent collection into the areas of your container garden that get dappled or morning sun.

FINE PRINT Prefers partial shade, and dry, well-drained soil. Fertilize monthly during the summer. Propagate most kalanchoe by tip or leaf cuttings anytime; in the case of devil's backbone, simply knock plantlets onto fresh soil. Overwinter in chilly or warm conditions with eastern, western, or southern exposure; provide low humidity and water when dry.

Lantana camara
SHRUB VERBENA

Lantana camara 'Lucky Peach'

Shrub | Zones 9 to 11

DESCRIPTION Knobs of clustered color wheel neighbors open outside-in on well-branched plants that have prickly stems and sandpapery deep green leaves. The inky berries that follow are meant to be admired, never eaten. In fact the entire plant is toxic to eat and may cause contact dermatitis. Never mind that (wear gloves to work with it) because nothing blooms with such abandon during the summer's hottest heat, and butterflies love it. Plant it in Crayola-crayon combinations with angel's trumpet, nicotiana, creeping Jenny, and New Zealand flax.

FINE PRINT Prefers full sun, and rich, moist soil. Prune in late summer if you see more berries than blooms, otherwise do not bother deadheading. Fertilize plants every two weeks from early to midsummer when grown in containers. Propagate by tip cuttings in summer. Overwinter in chilly conditions with southern or western exposure (water when dry and watch for aphids and whitefly) or dormant in dark storage, potted (keep soil just moist).

Lavandula
LAVENDER

Lavandula multifida and pineapple mint.

Perennial | Zones vary

DESCRIPTION French lavender (*L. dentata*, zones 8 to 10) grows small relaxed mounds of toothy gray leaves that are slightly fleshy and full of an oily turpentine-like perfume. Its pale lavender flowers are topped by purple bracts like tiny wings. Spanish or butterfly lavender (*L. stoechas*, zones 8 to 10) has darker purple flowers, very conspicuous wings, and a larger, even more lackadaisical, sprawling habit. Egyptian or fern-leaf lavender (*L. multifida*, zones 8 to 10) is the happy medium with tidy 18- to 24-in. clumps of gray lacy foliage and pale forked spikes of endless deep blue flowers. Plant lavender in containers or along sunny walkways frequented by family pets—all species are said to repel fleas.

FINE PRINT Prefers full sun, and dry, well-drained soil. Prune to shape in early spring or after blooming, taking care not to cut into old wood below green growth. Do not fertilize. Propagate by tip cuttings in spring. Overwinter in chilly conditions with southern or western exposure; water when dry.

MANDEVILLA

Sun Parasol Pretty Crimson *Mandevilla*

Vine | Zones 13 to 15

DESCRIPTION Brilliantly colored (bubblegum pink, white, yellow, or red), deep-throated, 3- to 4-in. propellers spin open from torpedo-shaped buds in a mad profusion all summer long. A climber with a low woody framework, mandevilla will snake its wires of deep green shiny leaves 4 to 6 ft. up a trellis and around the stems of neighboring plants but will be just as happy to dangle curls from a hanging basket. Give it its own container at the corner of the deck, at an entryway, or anywhere you can watch the hummingbirds get sucked in.

FINE PRINT Prefers full sun and moist soil. Fertilize every two weeks to a month during growth and flowering. Propagate by tip cuttings in spring and summer. Cut plant back by a one-third or one-half before overwintering in chilly or warm conditions with southern or western exposure; keep soil evenly moist. Or cut back to 12 in. and overwinter in dark storage, potted; keep soil just moist.

Mirabilis jalapa
FOUR O'CLOCK, MARVEL OF PERU

Mirabilis jalapa

Tuberous perennial | Zones 10 to 11

DESCRIPTION This old school, cottage garden favorite has creased, heart-shaped, grass-green leaves on succulent branches that grow 2 to 4 ft. tall, and garish hot pink, yellow, white, or striped and splotched miniature (1-in.) trumpets that release their fragrance and tempt the hummingbirds as temperatures drop in the evening. Peppercorn-sized seeds form in the flowers' place and drop into greedy palms or on the ground to germinate next summer. Plant them near the deck or windows that are left open at night.

FINE PRINT Prefers full sun and well-drained soil. Propagate by seed. No maintenance is necessary apart from editing out extra self-sown seedlings in spring. Overwinter in dark storage, bareroot in open containers or paper bags. Mist with water only if the tubers show signs of shriveling.

Nephrolepis exaltata
BOSTON FERN

Nephrolepis exaltata 'Tiger Fern'

Fern | Zones 9 to 11

DESCRIPTION Boston fern's great tufts (potentially growing to 7 ft. but more likely 3 to 4 ft. in confinement) of arching zigzagged fronds make any indoor or outdoor garden feel like a lush green jungle. For a change from plain green 'Bostoniensis', try yellow-and-green variegated 'Tiger Fern', chartreuse 'Rita's Gold', or 'Fluffy Ruffles' which displays deep green fronds with a finely cut, crunchy texture. Plant them in hanging pots (macramé is optional) and use them to decorate the porch or dangle from strong-limbed trees through the summer.

FINE PRINT Prefers bright shade (no direct sun), and moist, well-drained soil. Propagate by division or by allowing its leafless tendrils to land on fresh soil. Overwinter in chilly or warm conditions with any exposure; allow soil to dry slightly before watering.

Ocimum 'African Blue'
AFRICAN BLUE BASIL

Ocimum 'African Blue'

Perennial | Zones 9 to 11

DESCRIPTION The highly aromatic, purplish blue veined leaves on this 2 × 2 ft. plant—a hybrid cross of *O. kilimandscharicum* and *O basilicum* 'Dark Opal'—are decked in late summer with 6- to 12-in. long deep purple spires of lavender flowers beloved by honeybees. In the slanted light of fall, the glowing flowers and foliage pair perfectly with flowering ornamental grasses. Try the leaves in pesto for a piquant change from sweet basil, and the flowers in salads and cocktails.

FINE PRINT Prefers full sun, and average, moist, well-drained soil. Pinch plants to encourage branching. Propagate by tip cuttings in spring and late summer. Cut plants back by one-half to two-thirds before potting and bringing inside (or overwinter cuttings only). Provide chilly conditions with southern or eastern exposure; keep soil just moist and watch for aphids and whitefly.

Oxalis vulcanicola
SHAMROCK, SORREL

Oxalis 'Plum Crazy'

Perennial | Zones 9 to 11

DESCRIPTION Heart-shaped triads in unique shades of chartreuse, copper-orange, burgundy, black, and purple, grow into tightly knit sprawling, 6- to 8-in. tufts. Grow purple-and-black variegated 'Plum Crazy', or the chartreuse to orange 'Copper Glow' for their foliage alone but love their nonstop, fingernail-sized, banana-yellow flowers too. As luck would have it, these shamrocks do as well in containers, either alone or combined with coleus and New Guinea impatiens, as they would in the ground nestled along the front edge of borders with blue-flowering calamint and gray lamb's ear.

FINE PRINT Prefers full sun to partial shade, and moist to dry, well-drained soil. The more sun it gets, inside and out, the more intense the foliage color. Propagate by division or tip cuttings anytime. Overwinter in chilly or warm conditions with eastern, southern, or western exposure; water when dry.

Pelargonium
GERANIUM

Cuttings from scented geraniums, *Pelargonium* 'Lady Plymouth' and the peppermint *P. tomentosum*, forming calluses. Place the tips end-out in a plastic bag to keep their leaves from wilting.

Perennial | Zones vary

DESCRIPTION A garden without at least one of the nearly three hundred species would be like Christmas without gifts. The scalloped leaves of zonal geraniums (*P. zonale*, zones 9 to 11) display burgundy zones or multicolored variegations and bright clusters of summer flowers. Martha Washington or regal geraniums (*P. ×domesticum*, zones 10 to 11) have showier flowers triggered by long days and cool nights. Scented geraniums are beloved for foliage that comes in a perfumer's array from apple to rose to almond to peppermint, and are best planted near walkways or as pest-repelling companions for roses and vegetables. Pelargoniums grow anywhere from 4 in. to 3 ft., and look traditionally handsome with lavender, nicotiana, and salvia.

FINE PRINT Prefers full sun to partial shade, and moist to dry, well-drained soil. Propagate by tip cuttings, leaving stem ends exposed overnight to form a callus before sticking in medium. Cut plants back by half or more before bringing inside. Overwinter in chilly or warm conditions with southern or western exposure. Cut back again to a low framework in early spring. Water when dry year-round.

Pentas lanceolata
STAR CLUSTER

Pentas lanceolata 'Graffiti Pink'

Perennial | Zones 10 to 11

DESCRIPTION Nonstop clusters of cool pink (or white, magenta, or lavender) five-pointed stars sit on 1- to 2-ft. tightly branched shoulders of matte green leaves. Plant it in constellations with short nicotiana cultivars like 'Lime Green' and 'Crimson Bedder' and use its butterfly magnetism in the border front row with plumbago, tall verbena, and milkweed.

FINE PRINT Prefers full sun, and rich, well-drained soil. Propagate by tip cuttings in spring and late summer. Overwinter in chilly conditions with southern or western exposure; water when dry. Cut back by one-third to one-half in early spring as new growth breaks. Watch for aphids, whitefly, and spider mite.

Phormium

Phormium
NEW ZEALAND FLAX

Phormium 'Maori Sunrise'

Perennial | Zones 9 to 10

DESCRIPTION Clumps of 2- to 6-ft. long flat belt straps striped with green, cream, orange, pink or mahogany, depending on species and cultivar, give the eyes a slick landing zone and a vertical contrast more interesting than iris foliage could ever hope to be. Use New Zealand flax to modernize garden beds—even planted in the ground, their clumps are slow to increase—or leave them in containers as patio anchors. They may surprise you with a 6-ft. flower spike in spring or early summer.

FINE PRINT Prefers full sun to partial shade, and moist soil. Propagate by division, using a saw to get through the crown. Plants will tolerate light frost. Overwinter in chilly or warm conditions with any exposure except the darkest corners; water when dry.

Platycerium bifurcatum
STAGHORN FERN

Platycerium bifurcatum

Epiphytic fern | Zones 12 to 15

DESCRIPTION Long, forked tongues of gray-green fertile fronds with pale undersides arch out 1 to 3 ft. from layers of pale green disks (infertile fronds) that turn brown and papery. Make a trophy of its antlers by attaching it to a rot-resistant board (red cedar or white oak) that can be hung on a shady wall outside and displayed among pictures of safari inside; or pot it in well-draining potting mix to hang over the sink and from shady tree branches in summer.

FINE PRINT Prefers shade, high humidity, and frequent watering during summer (daily or every other day). To propagate, slice clusters apart. Watch for scale and scrape it off gently. Overwinter in warm conditions with any exposure out of direct sun; drench weekly.

Plectranthus ciliatus
SPUR FLOWER

A fall combination of *Plectranthus ciliatus* and shiso.

Perennial | Zones 10 to 11

DESCRIPTION I can hardly wait all summer for the lit-from-within purple autumn candelabras of spur flower and the spotted pale purple candles of *Plectranthus* 'Mona Lavender', which has bigger blooms but smaller, deeper green leaves. But with purple undersides to the quilted leaves and purple stems, both are striking, even out of bloom, especially with cousin coleus, and as a filler around hosta and under the legs of rice paper plant and Tiger Eyes staghorn sumac.

FINE PRINT Prefers partial shade and moist soil. Pinch to encourage branching. Propagate by tip cuttings in spring and late summer. Cut plants back by half to bring inside (or overwinter cuttings only) and provide cool conditions with eastern or western exposure; keep soil just moist; watch for aphids and whitefly.

Plectranthus scutellarioides
COLEUS

Perennial | Zones 10 to 12

DESCRIPTION An endless array of foliage shapes, colors, and patterns makes coleus one of the most used and abused "annuals." Often put to work as thrilling fillers in containers, they are just as happy working in the garden where they can be used to blaze color into dark and dapple shaded corners.

FINE PRINT Prefers partial shade to shade (but look for new cultivars that grow in full sun without scorching), and rich, moist, well-drained soil. Pinch growing tips to encourage branching and remove the flowers to direct attention back to the foliage. Propagate by tip cuttings anytime. Cut back by half before bringing inside. Overwinter in warm conditions with eastern or western exposure; water when dry; watch for aphids and whitefly. Prune again in early spring to a low framework.

A fall color combination of *Plectranthus scutellarioides* 'Freckles' and hakonechloa.

Rosmarinus officinalis
ROSEMARY

Rosmarinus officinalis

Shrub | Zones 8 to 11

DESCRIPTION My chef requests that I keep a rosemary plant growing for flavoring roasted chicken and root vegetables. Because rosemary's evergreen 2- to 4-ft. tall sprigs and twigs are deliciously aromatic, structurally handsome in the herb garden or on the deck, and its scent is said to enhance memory, I have no trouble remembering to oblige him. Tiny pale blue salvia-esque flowers decorate stem tips during spring captivity and again in fall.

FINE PRINT Prefers full sun and well-drained soil. Plants are drought tolerant once established in the ground; keep soil just moist when planted in a container. Propagate by tip cuttings in spring. Overwinter in chilly conditions with southern or western exposure; water when dry and prune as needed for your chef.

Salvia guaranitica
BLUE ANISE SAGE

Salvia guaranitica

Perennial | Zones 7 to 10

DESCRIPTION Small cobalt blue flowers like tiny sock puppets open in mid to late summer along one side of slender green stems that grow to 5 ft. tall and are densely packed with arrow-heads of grass-green leaves. The cultivar 'Black and Blue' has blackish calyxes and stems and a slightly shorter stature. Plant them wherever you can watch the neighborhood hummingbirds work every flower in late-summer combinations with apricot-colored dahlias and 'Nally's Lime Dot' false aster. Pineapple sage (*S. elegans*, zones 8 to 10) blooms much later but its 5-ft. tall fire engine–red spikes will flag down migrating hummingbirds on their way south, and meanwhile its generous mound of soft leaves is deliciously pineapple scented.

FINE PRINT Prefers full sun to partial shade, and moist soil. Spreads rhizomatously where hardy. Propagate by spring division or tip cuttings in early and late summer. Where marginally hardy, mulch the crown with shredded leaves and do not cut stems down to the ground until mid to late spring. Patience required: it is slow to emerge from dormancy. To overwinter indoors, cut back by half or all the way to the ground before placing in chilly conditions with southern or western exposure (watch for aphids and white fly) or in dark storage, potted; keep soil just moist either way.

Setaria palmifolia
PALM GRASS

Setaria palmifolia

Perennial grass | Zones 9 to 11

DESCRIPTION Wide, pointed, and delicately pleated lime-green spears arch 3 to 4 ft. with taller late-summer flower tassels, from a vigorously increasing clump of sturdy stalks. Palm grass leaves last well in water but are covered in a pelt of splintery filaments that lodge invisibly in finger skin so don't pick them without gloves on (or use a piece of tape to remove the splinters). Plant in tropical combinations with other equatorial plants like chocolate cosmos and amaranth.

FINE PRINT Prefers full sun to partial shade, and moist soil. Propagate by division in spring or fall. Cut stalks down to 6 to 12 in. and bring inside before the first frost. Overwinter potted plants in chilly conditions with any exposure or in dark storage; keep soil just moist either way.

Stachytarpheta mutabilis
PINK PORTERWEED, PINK SNAKEWEED

Stachytarpheta mutabilis 'Variegata'

Shrub | Zones 9 to 11

DESCRIPTION Tiny coral-pink funnels with tubes the size of a hummingbird's tongue climb weird snaking green 12- to 18-in. long stems in tight bunches. Well-branched plants grow between 3 and 6 ft. tall putting up dozens of flower stems at a time between 3- to 4-in. softly scratchy leaves. Give it or its purple-flowered sister (*S. urticifolia*) a wide berth in the middle or back of a bed planted with other attractive plants like blue anise sage and nicotiana, and rice paper plant for contrast.

FINE PRINT Prefers full sun and well-drained soil. Propagate by tip cuttings in spring and late summer. Pot up mature plants, cutting them back by half to two-thirds (or overwinter cuttings only) and provide chilly conditions with southern, eastern, or western exposure. Keep soil just moist throughout winter and prune again to lowest dormant leaf buds in early spring.

Tibouchina urvilleana

GLORY BUSH, PRINCESS FLOWER

Tibouchina urvilleana

Shrub | Zones 13 to 15

DESCRIPTION Red-edged, creased velvet leaves and red fuzzy stems are reason enough to add this large shrub (to 10 ft. or more) to your collection, never mind the luminous open-faced purple flowers that arrive in succession from mid to late summer. But if its 3- to 6-in. arrow-shaped leaves aren't showy enough, grow *T. heteromalla*, which has slightly inflated looking paddles up to 10-in. long and is topped by 1-ft. tall spires of red-centered purple flowers. Either plant will be a stunner in the container garden, popping against bright red mandevilla and the straps of cabbage palm and New Zealand flax.

FINE PRINT Prefers full sun, and rich, moist soil. You can prune these shrubs hard—even to just above the lowest leaf nodes—to keep size manageable. Propagate by tip cuttings in spring or late summer. Overwinter potted plants in dark storage, or in chilly or warm conditions with southern or western exposure; keep soil just moist either way.

Uncinia uncinata 'Rubra'

RED HOOK SEDGE

Perennial | Zones 8 to 11

DESCRIPTION The grass isn't always greener. Roughly curled and folded russet blades erupt out of a dense 12 × 12 in. clump and send up dark flower spikes in late summer. One red hook sedge would be pretty enough as a garnet pendant in a container but a beaded necklace strung around the garden would be even lovelier. Let it contrast with extra-leafy leaves like bergenia and lettuces or nest it alongside fellow partial-shade moisture-loving plants like astilbes and plumbago.

FINE PRINT Prefers partial shade to shade (especially where summers bake), and cool, moist soil. Comb out dead leaves in spring; do not cut back. Propagate by division in spring. Overwinter in chilly conditions with any exposure; keep soil just moist.

Uncinia uncinata 'Rubra'

IN SUM

NOT ALL OF US ARE BORN garden designers. I know I'm not. But I also don't think we have to be (so cut yourself some slack) because something pretty great happens as we get more excited about gardening. When we take our chances with plants that *grow*—plants that place themselves into inspiring combinations, supply plenty of extras to play around with, and outlive their first season; when we participate fully and make the most of a living process that is never "done," we learn the art by doing, naturally.

Even though I have become as hooked on that process as I am to breathing, I also firmly believe that it should be fun. Only then will the garden be wildly entertaining, physically exhilarating, exquisitely exhausting, and truly beautiful from one moment to the next. I also believe that your garden should fit your life. It should provide a meditative pastime, a creative outlet, and a demanding challenge that cultivates confidence along with roots, shoots, stems, leaves, and flowers. I can only hope you'll agree and feel readier now than ever to dig in and let nature do its thing.

If so, look around your garden and your life and tally up. You'll inevitably see a wealth of resources within reach. And now that you know how to take advantage of prolific plants, as well as your climate, the sunlit and dark corners of your house, the strength of your arms, and most of all your own imagination, I trust you'll use that treasure trove to grow the garden of your dreams. And then pass it on.

A collection of containers on my potting bench ready to accept and deploy the garden's extras.

REFERENCES AND RESOURCES

NO ONE GARDENS ALONE. Not when there are plant societies and garden clubs to join; beautifully written and photographed magazines to discover; newspaper columns to read; an international community of garden bloggers to follow; and books by passionate kindred spirits to stack on our potting benches and nightstands. The list in this section is by no means a complete catalog of all of my favorite references, rather, a small compilation of relevant further reading, and those that I reread as I wrote this book.

As exciting and inspiring as the pictures, methods, and opinions are in print and electronic media, they are no substitute for personally experiencing the sensory overload of a living, blooming, buzzing, constantly changing garden. Use your own local public garden as a resource to see how plants grow in your area through the seasons and take their best ideas home. For an invitation into spectacular private gardens, join the Garden Conservancy (www.gardenconservancy.org), and/or check their annual Open Days listing for unlocked gates nearby. Add far-flung gardens to your vacation itinerary by using the Garden and Landscape Guide (www.gardenvisit.com) or the National Gardening Association's Public Gardens Locator (www.garden.org/public_garden) to map your route.

Although I always recommend shopping at local independent garden centers for plants adapted to thrive in your garden's climate, I have included a selection of mail-order nurseries and seed companies who offer irresistibly interesting choices, a wealth of information, and terrific customer service.

Great Reads

Armitage, Allan M. 2004. *Armitage's Garden Annuals: A Color Encyclopedia*. Portland, OR: Timber Press.

Baggett, Pam. 2008. *¡Tropicalismo! Spice Up Your Garden with Cannas, Bananas, and 93 Other Eye-Catching Tropical Plants*. Portland, OR: Timber Press.

Ballard, Ernesta Drinker. 1971. *Growing Plants Indoors: A Garden in Your House*. Illustrated, revised 1973. New York: Barnes & Noble Books.

Brickell, Christopher and H. Marc Cathey, eds. 1996. *American Horticultural Society A–Z Encyclopedia of Garden Plants*. Revised US ed. 2004. New York. DK Publishing.

Burrell, C. Colston. 2011. *Native Alternatives to Invasive plants*. Guides for a Greener Planet, Handbook 185. Ed. Janet Marinelli, Bonnie Harper-Lore. 3rd ed. Brooklyn, NY: Brooklyn Botanic Garden.

Capon, Brian. 2010. *Botany for Gardeners*. 3rd ed. Portland, OR: Timber Press.

Culp, David. 2012. *The Layered Garden: Design Lessons for Year-Round Beauty from Brandywine Cottage*. Portland, OR: Timber Press.

DiSabato-Aust, Tracy. 2006. *The Well-Tended Perennial Garden: Planting and Pruning Techniques*. Expanded edition. Portland, OR: Timber Press.

Druse, Ken. 2012. *Making More Plants: The Science, Art, and Joy of Propagation*. 1st ed. New York: Clarkson Potter, 2000. Reprint, Stewart, Tabori & Chang.

Eck, Joe and Wayne Winterrowd. 2009. *Our Life in Gardens*. 2nd ed. 2010. New York: Farrar, Straus and Giroux.

Hadden, Evelyn. 2012. *Beautiful No-Mow Yards: 50 Amazing Lawn Alternatives*. Portland, OR: Timber Press.

Jennings, Karen Park. 2006. *Park's Success with Seed*. Greenwood, SC: Park Seed Company.

Keys, Andrew. 2012. *Why Grow That When You Can Grow This?: 255 Extraordinary Alternatives to Everyday Problem Plants*. Portland, OR: Timber Press.

Kowalchik, Claire and William H. Hylton, eds. 1987. *Rodale's Illustrated Encyclopedia of Herbs*. 2nd ed. 1998. Emmaus, PA: Rodale Press.

Johnson, Wendy. 2008. *Gardening at the Dragon's Gate: At Work in the Wild and Cultivated World*. New York. Bantam Dell.

Lloyd, Christopher. 2005. *Succession Planting for Year-Round Pleasure*. Portland, OR: Timber Press. ——. 1984. *The Well-Chosen Garden*. New York: Harper & Row.

Lloyd, Christopher and Graham Rice. 1994. *Garden Flowers from Seed*. 2nd ed. 1995. Portland, OR: Timber Press.

Lowenfels, Jeff and Wayne Lewis. 2010. *Teaming with Microbes*. Portland, OR: Timber Press.

Martin, Tovah. 1994. *Well-Clad Windowsills: Houseplants for Four Exposures*. New York: Macmillan. ——, 2012. *The Unexpected Houseplant: 220 Extraordinary Choices for Every Spot in Your Home*. Portland: Timber Press.

McGowan, Alice and Brian McGowan. 2008. *Bulbs in the Basement, Geraniums on the Windowsill: How to Grow & Overwinter 165 Tender Plants*. North Adams, MA: Storey Publishing.

Messervy, Julie Moir. 2009. *Home Outside: Creating the Landscape you Love*. Newtown, CT: Taunton Press.

Mitchell, Henry. 1981. *The Essential Earthman*. Bloomington, IN: Indiana University Press. Reprint, Houghton Mifflin Company.

Spencer-Jones, Rae, Ed. 2007. *1001 Gardens You Must See Before You Die*. Hauppauge, NY: Barron's Educational Series.

Stein, Sarah. 1993. *Noah's Garden: Restoring the Ecology of our own Backyards*. New York. Houghton Mifflin Company.

Tallamy, Douglas W. 2007. *Bringing Nature Home: How You Can Sustain Wildlife with Native Plants*. 2nd ed. 2009. Portland, OR: Timber Press.

Thompson, Peter. 1993. *The Propagator's Handbook: Fifty Foolproof Recipes—Hundreds of Plants for your Garden*. 2nd ed. 1996. North Pomfret, VT: Trafalgar Square Publishing.

Xerces Society. 2011. *Attracting Native Pollinators: Protecting North America's Bees and Butterflies*. North Adams, MA: Storey Publishing.

Plant and Seed Sources

Annie's Annuals & Perennials
801 Chesley Avenue
Richmond, CA 94801
888-266-4370
www.anniesannuals.com

Avant Gardens
710 High Hill Road
Dartmouth, MA 02747
508-998-8819
www.avantgardensne.com

Chiltern Seeds
Crowmarsh Battle Barns, 114
Preston Crowmarsh
Wallingford, OX10 6SL, England
+44 (0)1491-824675
www.chilternseeds.co.uk

Cistus Nursery
22711 NW Gillihan Road
Portland, OR 97231
503-621-2233
www.cistus.com

Digging Dog Nursery
31101 Middle Ridge Road
Albion, CA 95410
707-937-1130
www.diggingdog.com

Far Reaches Farm
1818 Hastings Avenue
Port Townsend, WA 98368
360-385-5114
www.farreachesfarm.com

Logee's Greenhouses
141 North Street
Danielson, CT 06239
888-330-8038
www.logees.com

Plant Delights Nursery
9241 Sauls Road
Raleigh, NC 27603
919-772-4794
www.plantdelights.com

Renee's Garden
6060 Graham Hill Road
Felton, CA 95018
888-880-7228
www.reneesgarden.com

Select Seeds
180 Stickney Hill Road
Union, CT 06076
800-684-0395
www.selectseeds.com

Stokes
296 Collier Road S
Thorold, ON, Canada
800-396-9238
www.stokeseeds.com

Thompson & Morgan
Poplar Lane
Ipswich, Suffolk, UK IP8 3BU
800-274-7333
www.tmseeds.com (US sales)
www.thompson-morgan.com (UK sales)

METRIC CONVERSIONS

inches	centimeters
½	1.3
1	2.5
2	5.1
3	7.6
4	10
5	13
6	15
7	18
8	20
9	23
10	25
12	30
18	46
20	51
24	61
30	76

feet	meters
1	0.3
2	0.6
3	0.9
4	1.2
5	1.5
6	1.8
7	2.1
8	2.4
9	2.7
10	3.0
12	3.6
15	4.5
20	6.0
25	7.5
30	9.0

temperatures

$$°C = 5/9 \times (°F - 32)$$
$$°F = (9/5 \times °C) + 32$$

PLANT HARDINESS ZONES

Average Annual Minimum Temperature

ZONE	temperature (°F)			temperature (°C)		
1	Below		-50	Below		-46
2	-50	to	-40	-46	to	-40
3	-40	to	-30	-40	to	-34
4	-30	to	-20	-34	to	-29
5	-20	to	-10	-29	to	-23
6	-10	to	0	-23	to	-18
7	0	to	10	-18	to	-12
8	10	to	20	-12	to	-7
9	20	to	30	-7	to	-1
10	30	to	40	-1	to	4
11	40	to	50	4	to	10
12	50	to	60	10	to	16
13	60	to	70	16	to	21

Plant hardiness data for the United States: http://planthardiness.ars.usda.gov/PHZMWeb/
Plant hardiness data for Canada: http://www.planthardiness.gc.ca/

ACKNOWLEDGMENTS

I HAVE HAD THE PRIVILEGE to study at the boots of masters. I owe Julie Morris, Blithewold's director of horticulture emerita, and Gail Read, gardens manager, the moon for the chance to gain confidence and voice alongside them in Blithewold's gardens and greenhouse. I learn something new every day, and more from the garden volunteers there than they might think possible. And I feel incredibly lucky for every minute I spend with expert gardeners and industry professionals, far too numerous to mention by name, who make plant parenthood look easy. My deepest thanks go to Phillip Schwab for encouraging a growing enthusiasm and letting me call his garden my first.

I am beyond grateful to my faithful blog and column readers, especially author Andrew Keys who paid me the biggest compliment ever, and Beverly Christ. Thanks to my proofreaders, Gary Martin and Patricia Green whose goofy notes in the margins made rewriting more fun. I owe Julie Morris another moon for checking the content for horticultural correctness. (Any remaining errors snuck in after.) If not for the team at Timber Press, you wouldn't even be reading these words. I am especially grateful to Juree Sondker, who so gracefully guided this project from proposal to print, uncluttering my messy thought process along the way, and Mollie Firestone for taking such tremendous care with the manuscript.

I have Marci LeBrun and her constructive criticism to thank for making me a better photographer. For allowing me to take my best shots, a huge round of applause goes to Patricia Bailey and the Hope Street Blooms kids; Gioia Browne and Jim Marsh; Martha Christina; Sean Conway; Layanee DeMerchant; Jim Donahue of Green Animals Topiary Garden in Portsmouth, Rhode Island; Tim and Leila Gillespie; Pamela Gilpin; Lois Hartley; Andrew Keys; Byron and Laurelynn Martin of Logee's Greenhouse in Danielson, Connecticut; Heidi McCabe; Pam Meyer; Julie Morris; Jill Nooney and Bob Munger of Bedrock Gardens in Lee, New Hampshire; Cris and Eric Offenburg; Rick Peckham of Peckham's Greenhouse in Little Compton, Rhode Island; Virginia Purviance; Louis Raymond; Gail Read; Dorothy Swift; Katherine and Chris Tracey of Avant Gardens in Dartmouth, Massachusetts; Margaret Whitehead; and Laura Willson. I used those photo shoots as much for inspiration as for pictures, though I'm thrilled some made it into the book. Thanks also to Karen Binder, Blithewold's executive director for allowing me to use the photos I take for Blithewold's garden blog. Layanee DeMerchant, Gail Read, and Phillip Schwab deserve extra thanks for contributing their own photos to help fill my gaps.

I credit my family and friends, especially Mum and Gary, Miki Green, Anna Links, and May Morris for giving me the push of love and encouragement that sent me leaping out of my comfort zone to write this. You're (all) The Best. And finally, there aren't words enough to acknowledge my husband, chef, love, Isaiah Lawrence and the million ways he works to make my work easier, and our life together as smooth and sweet as his signature crème brûlée.

PHOTOGRAPHY CREDITS

Photography credits appear on page 213.

Published in 2014 by Timber Press, Inc.

The Haseltine Building
133 S.W. Second Avenue, Suite 450
Portland, Oregon 97204-3527
timberpress.com

6a Lonsdale Road
London NW6 6RD
timberpress.co.uk

Printed in China
Book design by Jane Jeszeck/Jigsaw, www.jigsawseattle.com

Library of Congress Cataloging-in-Publication Data

Green, Kristin.
Plantiful: start small, grow big with 150 plants that spread, self-sow, and
overwinter/Kristin Green.—First ed.
      p. cm.
Includes bibliographical references and index.
ISBN 978-1-60469-387-4
1. Gardening. 2. Plant propagation. I. Title. II. Title: Start small, grow
big with 150 plants that spread, self-sow, and overwinter.
SB453.G794 2014
635—dc23   2013019896

A catalog record for this book is also available from the British Library.

INDEX

ISAIAH LAWRENCE

ABOUT THE AUTHOR

KRISTIN GREEN first unearthed a passion for gardening while on the West Coast earning degrees in art and painting from the University of Washington. Now back on native soil, she is a full-time, year-round gardener serving as interpretive horticulturist, garden blogger, and photographer at Blithewold Mansion, Gardens & Arboretum, a 33-acre non-profit public garden in Bristol, Rhode Island. She is also head gardener and curator of plants for her own .17-acre estate, where she writes a regular column called Down to Earth for local newspapers, and blogs, irregularly, at trenchmanicure. wordpress.com. Her writing and photographs have been published in *Fine Gardening* and other magazines.